INSIGHT IS 20/20

INSIGHT IS 20/20

HOW TO TRUST YOURSELF
TO PROTECT YOURSELF
FROM NARCISSISTIC ABUSE
& TOXIC RELATIONSHIPS

CHELLI PUMPHREY, MA, LPC

NEW DEGREE PRESS

COPYRIGHT © 2022 CHELLI PUMPHREY, MA, LPC
All rights reserved.

INSIGHT IS 20/20
How to Trust Yourself to Protect Yourself from Narcissistic Abuse & Toxic Relationships

ISBN   979-8-88504-910-8 *Paperback*
       979-8-88504-619-0 *Kindle Ebook*
       979-8-88504-169-0 *Ebook*

To Mila and Marley, may you love with an open heart, a wise mind, and a fiercely protective spirit.

To the memory of my mom, Cindy Pumphrey. Without you, this book wouldn't exist. And yes, I will continue to love like I've never been hurt.

To anyone who has been scarred by love, stay strong. Love has not hurt you. Someone who doesn't know how to love hurt you. Always remember the difference.

You always know.

CONTENTS

	FOREWORD BY SANDRA L. BROWN, MA	11
	INTRODUCTION	19
PART I.	**EXTERNAL RED FLAGS: UNDERSTANDING PATHOLOGY**	**37**
CHAPTER 1.	RED FLAGS	39
CHAPTER 2.	PATHOLOGY 101	55
CHAPTER 3.	THE FACES OF NARCISSISM	71
CHAPTER 4.	MINDFUCKERY	85
PART II.	**INTERNAL RED FLAGS: THE BODY SPEAKS YOUR TRUTH**	**101**
CHAPTER 5.	WHAT MAKES US VULNERABLE?	103
CHAPTER 6.	THE #1 RED FLAG	119
CHAPTER 7.	THE BODY SPEAKS YOUR TRUTH: THE LANGUAGE OF TRAUMA	135
CHAPTER 8.	THE LANGUAGE OF ATTACHMENT	151
CHAPTER 9.	THE BODY SPEAKS YOUR TRUTH: THE LANGUAGE OF DISEASE	165
PART III.	**EMPOWERED ACTION**	**181**
CHAPTER 10.	HEALING: THE FIRST STEPS	183
CHAPTER 11.	HOW TO LISTEN	199
	CONCLUSION	225
	RESOURCES FOR HELP & HEALING	231
	APPENDIX	235
	ACKNOWLEDGMENTS	245

FOREWORD BY SANDRA L. BROWN, MA

It is 2022, and only recently have 'Pathological Love Relationships' (called PLRs—often referred to as narcissistic and psychopathic abuse) hit our societal *awareness*. I am always amazed that this specific field of recognizing the most dangerous disorders in the *DSM, a*nd what they can do to others relationally, is only *fifteen years old*. In psychology theory history, we are a neophyte.

Thirty years ago, it was incomprehensible to me that in the field of psychology, the relationships that were the *most* harmful, the *most* traumatizing, and the *most* dangerous had flown under the radar of the field's recognition and importantly, *differentiation* from other types of dysfunctional and abusive relationships. I was a brand-new therapist working with personality disordered (PD) clients, searching for information about the types of relationships I was witnessing as my PD clients brought their survivor-partners to session because of relationship problems. While I was also a trauma therapist trained in domestic violence, the survivor-partners of my PD clients were a far cry from what I was taught in domestic violence.

The problem trio called 'The Dark Triad,' are the disorders of narcissistic and antisocial personality disorders and, additionally, psychopathy. These disorders make up the annals of history…and often criminal science. These dark and antagonistic (yet often charming and law-abiding) personalities have held captive the minds of researchers for eons. Millions of dollars each year are spent, for instance, on studying 'the psychopathic mind,' but there was not one paper, one study, nor one mention of the personal relationships with their intimate partner victims.

I searched for years for information about the relationships when one of the partners has 'personality pathology or disorders.' I looked for what were typical relational dynamics, what happened to the survivor as a result, and how does one work with this type of trauma? There was nothing—no professional journal articles, no books, no research, not even a word describing the type of relationships these were. They were simply assumed to be domestic violence, with the same type of abusers, victims, dynamics, and resulting harm.

Over the course of the first fourteen years as a therapist in the absence of any data, I worked at gathering information on the survivors for my own understanding so that treatment could be specific to what they experienced. I had no way of knowing that I was pioneering a new psychological wilderness. I was just a frustrated therapist in dire need of figuring out what pathological people '*do*' to the people they claim to love.

While I had spent a lot of years 'gaining' knowledge about abusive relationships through training, I had to ironically, 'let go' of many of the dynamics I was taught in domestic violence and embrace the repeating stories and representations of 'these' relationships the survivors described. I realized that if anyone had studied these relationships separately from the over-arching theory of domestic violence, the information would be out there. But it wasn't. I had to start from scratch.

I mounted a huge whiteboard on my office wall and would draw with arrows, circles, and cycles, the relational dynamics that seemed unique to these relationships as described by survivors. I would add to the drawings over many years trying to arrive at an understanding of the dynamics involved with some of the most dangerous of all disorders. Many of the trauma assessments I had been trained to use had to be discarded. I had to develop trauma surveys and various assessments trying to get to the bottom of what made these relationships so different and so inevitably harmful. Likewise, I had to 'tweak' trauma treatment for them focusing on unique aspects that were completely different from my run-of-the-mill domestic violence clients or even my typical PTSD clients.

Instead, I collected data and studied the survivor's profile that was different from a standard domestic violence survivor. I had to also 'let go' of labels that had been applied to them as 'codependent, dependent, and a victim of learned helplessness' that were not applicable to a surprisingly large amount of the survivors. I had to challenge much of what I had been taught about these survivor's trauma and history, because many of these survivors did not have adverse childhoods or a 'traumatic history,' a common assumption.

In essence, I had to learn anew.

Finally, in 2005, I wrote 'a' chapter about these relationships in my book, *How to Spot a Dangerous Man,* introducing the concept of 'pathological relationships.' Later in 2007, our next book, *Women Who Love Psychopaths: Inside the Relationships of Inevitable Harm with Psychopaths, Sociopaths, & Narcissists* was a full-length book focused on these pathological relationships and was considered to be the 'seminal' book—the first book of its kind that unveiled our current naming and understanding of these relationships with cluster Bs and psychopaths. As we studied and became involved in collegiate research with Purdue University about the survivors, we updated our findings in the book's additional editions in 2009 and 2018, challenging the concept of codependency.

A mere fifteen years ago, there was no recognition of PLRs as a 'type' of relationship—no label, or descriptions, or theory, and no treatment approach for recovery. Consequently, there were no therapists hanging out a shingle for this when its concept did not yet exist. Today, a short decade and a half after the concept's unveiling, Google results for 'narcissistic abuse' lists over 11 million results for this relational concept. Clearly, it was a concept whose time had come.

Over thirty years, our work has been to unearth the *science* about these relationships. As a complex interweave of different fields of psychology, it meant tying together the fields of psychopathology, personality science, and complex trauma to create this new genre of counseling. And since the psychology field is not easily convinced, it also meant developing what the field holds dear—a theory, relational dynamics, a profile of the survivor, an understanding of how their trauma is different through trauma studies, and a treatment approach for them that was evidenced-based and trauma-informed. Then there was the necessity of accumulating a 'history' of using this information in treatment that actually works. That accumulation took decades.

Since our book's release, the survivor's need for evidenced-based, trauma-informed, and unique PLR- focused treatment has never been more prevalent. Survivors resonated with the description of this type of relationship and traumatic experience. Similar to the early days of the domestic violence field development, PLRs became a grassroots movement of survivors spreading the word. In the absence of many trained therapists, survivors took the ball and ran with it. They began websites, blogs, books, YouTube channels—preaching the everlasting message of pathological relationships. Without the psychological training in what I have referenced as a 'complex interweave' of three fields of psychology, survivors began offering services without training or education.

Today, 11 million Google results bares very little resemblance to the science, theory, or recovery methods that were developed. This complicated science has been reduced to simplistic and unproven approaches. Into a field with very little competent care came well-meaning survivors with an experience of trauma that was used as the totality of an approach in an area that requires education and training in psychopathology, personality science, and complex trauma. This makes the teaching and the understanding of the real science necessary to re-educate both survivor and therapist from what has been widely and errantly proclaimed. I'd like to say the road to where we are today was smooth sailing. However, it hasn't been due to so much misinformation by survivors unequipped about a complex and complicated topic about the traumatic injury in others.

That makes *this* book very important. The book you hold in your hands, *Insight is 20/20,* is part of the journey to bring trauma-informed, knowledgeable, and effective healing to your unique experience. What has been desperately needed are professionals who understand the pathology of the partner, the survivor's personality risk, complex trauma and attachment theory, and recovery methods that are based on more than 'a' personalized experience. Chelli Pumphrey's book is a necessary and welcomed approach in a sea of misinformation and science-less and errant approaches.

In 2017, The Association for NPD/Psychopathy Survivor Treatment, Research & Education was formed to bring our decades of science, research, and complex interweaving of three fields of psychology to therapists for an evidenced-based and effective treatment approach. Chelli, as a PLR survivor, brings a personalized knowledge of these relationships combined with the clinical and real science of the aftermath that is consistent with The Association's research. This book is the delicate balance of *experience* and *education* of the 'complex interweave.'

- She brings correction to what has occurred in the 11 million Google results that imply all abuse is 'narcissistic' abuse.
- She educates us on why even the use of the word 'narcissistic abuse' is too narrow.

- She helps survivors and therapists understand the foundation of personality disorders/psychopathy behind the traumatic aftermath.
- She addresses the misconceptions about 'codependency.'
- And she brings fresh insights into the survivors 'hallmark feature' of cognitive dissonance.

Importantly for survivor *and* therapist, she brings her personal *and* therapeutic insights into recovery methods that are sure to help survivors begin their healing journey.

Insight Is 20/20 is what has been tragically absent in this book genre that is drowning in a sea of '*My Life With a Narcissist*' type of books which we call '*the traumatic memoir*,' which may bring the survivor some awareness, but is also highly triggering for a traumatized survivor to read to begin their educational journey. This book, with its gentle, trauma-informed approach to awareness and education, gives survivors what they need to understand their experience, while sparing them a traumatic reaction from reading it. Chelli is, after all, a trauma therapist.

To continue to grow this relational concept, we must elevate those writers who truly understand PLRs not only in theory, but in truth and accuracy. One of our studies highlighted how effective accurate pathology education was for survivors in reducing their intrusive thoughts and cognitive dissonance. This makes accuracy, like in *Insight Is 20/20, therapeutic.*

Our arduous journey to bring the concept of PLRs to societal awareness, and more importantly to a survivor's needed education, should not end in misinformation. The entire reason for creating this field was to meet the survivor's need for professional, effective, evidenced-based, and trauma-informed recovery. We have fought too many decades for this to be recognized and accepted as a true relational concept to allow it to be discredited and dismissed as survivor pop psychology by professionals and accepted as accurate by survivors.

To that end, this book claims its rightful place in science, traumatology, and recovery.

Much Healing,
Sandra L. Brown, MA

The Institute for Relational Harm Reduction & Public Pathology Education

President of The Association for NPD/Psychopathy Survivor Treatment, Research & Education

INTRODUCTION

"I need you to give me lots of hugs today," he whispered in a voice that sounded childlike and sweet as honey. To an outside observer, it might have sounded like an innocent request, but I sensed the venom beneath it. My body bristled at my typical morning greeting from Tom, my partner for the last three years. I froze as I felt a rush of heat course through my body along with my pounding heart. Ignoring every instinct to jump out of bed and run, I rolled toward him, as if I had become a robot. I knew I had to act quick, as any pause would have meant I was disinterested in compliance. With the skill of a puppeteer, I forced every muscle in my body to soften, embrace, and soothe him, while my mouth uttered empty words dressed up in empathy, rainbows, and butterflies. "Of course, I'll give you hugs today. I love you."

I armored myself, afraid to breathe as I waited for his response. I felt his body stiffen as he held his arms to his sides, never rolling toward me or lifting his arms to hug me back. "I need it to be a deeper hug. And I don't want to ask for it. I need you to come up behind me and hug me when I'm not expecting it several times a day. Can you try again?" I nestled my head into his chest, mostly to hide the swelling tears in my eyes, and strengthened my grip on him but his arms remained at his side, as he received my hug without an ounce of reciprocation. "Thank you. I really needed that," he said in a sing-song voice as he rose from the bed.

I collapsed into silent tears in my pillow as my mind floated back to the beginning, when I showered him in affection. I have always been an affectionate person, yet I now felt repulsed by his touch and would instinctually withdraw when he approached me. I made my way to the bathroom and looked at myself in the mirror. I had dark circles under my eyes from constant insomnia. I no longer recognized my body after gaining twenty pounds in the last year with him. My body ached, my muscles and joints were rigid and painful. My gut was a wreck. Most days I felt like I was living in a fog and found it difficult to concentrate and make decisions. My heart ached with regret, confusion, and grief.

He never laid a hand on me. There were no bruises or broken bones that might have alerted my friends and family. This wasn't the movie version of a battered wife planning her escape in the middle of the night with nothing but the clothes on her back, where people would understand why she left. Instead, I feared that his friends likely believed *I was the crazy one,* not only because he told them stories to make them believe it, but because he appeared to be a kind, loving, stable person to outsiders. No one would believe he was a narcissist since he acted so "normal." I had no scars to prove what I was experiencing, as it was simply a slow whittling away of my heart and psyche. It was more subtle than obvious, more passive than aggressive. That unreciprocated hug spoke volumes. It was my job to give, to please, to make him happy, and to ensure he always felt special and admired. The catch: I was to expect nothing in return.

The worst part was not this heartbreak, nor the emotional and psychological abuse I experienced. The worst part was realizing this pattern was familiar. It started with dysfunctional family dynamics in childhood along with a narcissistic stepparent which led to having several partners with varying degrees of narcissism over the years. I realized this man, whom I once believed was my soul mate, who once seemed so tender-hearted, loving, and self-aware, was also a narcissist.

He was different from the others though, which is why I missed the signs, even as a therapist who specializes in working with narcissistic abuse. I discovered he had a more subtle yet even more toxic form of this disorder, called vulnerable or covert narcissism. I fell for his charade of humility. I saw his woundedness and dismissed early red flags due to being strongly guided by my compassion and empathy. He didn't wear his narcissism on his sleeve like the others. He wore it in his empathy depraved heart, disguised by a cloak of vulnerability, kindness, and generosity.

My mind was spinning with questions. *How did I miss the red flags? Why did I dismiss the red flags that I saw? He seemed so different! Chelli, you did so much healing and work to stop this pattern! What in the hell? And you're a therapist! You should have known better!*

The truth is, the red flags were there from the beginning. They were subtle and confusing, or I misinterpreted them altogether, yet they were there. It wasn't until we were deep into the relationship and had joined our lives together that I could see the bigger picture. *The mask came off* and I saw his true self. I was devastated when I realized I could have prevented this painful entanglement had I only trusted the red flags I saw within weeks of dating. All I could do was accept this reality and begin to extract myself from the relationship, despite the pain and challenges it created. Leaving was nothing compared to the lifetime of trauma I would have endured if I stayed. However, this time I was determined to understand why I kept finding myself in these relationships so that it never happened again.

HINDSIGHT IS 20/20, OR IS IT?

In my work as a therapist, there are two questions that every single survivor of narcissistic or relational abuse has shared with me: *How did I miss the red flags? Or why did I ignore the red flags?* The bitter taste of regret can shake you to your core when you realize you could have prevented so much pain, had you only known what to look for and how to actually trust the red flags. The wasted time, the heartbreak, the loss, the irreparable damage–it can sometimes feel as painful as the abuse itself. When you look back over time, you will usually see there were clear warning signs, or perhaps a pattern of early but subtle signs that eventually became a glaring red flag telling you that this Prince or Princess Charming was now Prince or Princess Harming. Usually by this point, you are in deep enough that it will, at the minimum, break your heart, or, at worst, cost you your lifestyle, your finances, your children, your job, or even your life, in order to leave. When we feel this guilt and shame for missing and ignoring the red flags that could have steered us away from an abusive partner, we continue to experience the afterglow of abuse, long after we leave the relationship.

They say, "hindsight is 20/20," right? But what if you didn't need to wait until after the fact? What if you could develop clear vision that helped you identify if a partner was a narcissist, psychopath, or manipulative individual before you fell in love, moved in, shared finances, had that baby, married, or spent precious years of your life with them? This is possible, and I'm going to teach you how to do this. However, before we talk about how to prevent these relationships, we must first identify what they are.

UNDERSTANDING NARCISSISM AND PERSONALITY DISORDERS

Is it me or is everyone a *narcissist* these days? It seems the term "narcissist" has become a buzz word to describe everyone's ex-partner, boss, or even a president. It seems the term made its way into mainstream conversations between 2016 and 2020, with former US President Donald Trump, as many identified his grandiose, empathy lacking behaviors as "narcissistic." I had countless clients come into sessions telling me he reminded them of their parent, boss, or partner, and they realized they might be dealing with a narcissist in their personal life. In fact, googling the phrase, "is my partner a narcissist?" brings up about 9,790,000 results. There must be a reason for the rise in interest in this disorder.

Current statistics from the *Diagnostic and Statistical Manual of Mental Disorders* (DSM-5) suggest 1 percent of the

US population actually meets the criteria for narcissistic personality disorder (NPD), and 16 percent of the clinical population (people in the mental health system) meet this criteria. Of these groups, 50–75 percent are male (American Psychiatric Association, 2013). These statistics perplexed me. Have we just fallen in love with a trendy word that describes self-centered people, or are these statistics inaccurate?

Current research has not provided us a clear answer to this question. In their book, *The Narcissism Epidemic*, Keith Campbell, PhD and Jean Twenge, PhD challenge the claim that narcissism is a rare phenomenon. They estimate 1 in 16, or 6 percent of Americans have actually experienced diagnosable narcissistic personality disorder at some point in their lifetime, and their research has shown a 2 percent increase in narcissism in the last couple of decades. A large-scale study done in 2008 by researchers at the National Institutes of Health, found that 9.4 percent of Americans in their twenties had experienced NPD at some point in their life, compared with only 3.2 percent of people over sixty-five.

Researchers look toward recent cultural influences that have fueled this epidemic, including the "selfie generation." Social media has created a trend with younger generations who are posting more selfies, sharing intimate details of their lives, and are focused on how many likes or views they get on their posts. Rates of self-esteem in young people have increased over the last few decades. Researchers have also found an increase in pronouns "I" and "me" used more frequently than "we" and "us" in literature. From song lyrics to tv shows, there is a growing trend to be more self-focused and oriented toward fame (Vater, Moritz, and Roepk, 2018).

Despite this data, there is other research that claims to have found no evidence of an increase of narcissism over time and see the 2 percent increase as statistically insignificant (Trzesniewski & Donnellan, 2010). One must question whether the heightened focus on the term has increased only because we have social media and the internet available to spread these ideas throughout the public psyche.

It's important to understand the nature of personality disorders in general, so we can better understand narcissism and its place in this book. The *Diagnostic and Statistical Manual of Mental Disorders* (*DSM-5*) defines a personality disorder as "a way of thinking, feeling and behaving that deviates from the expectations of the culture, causes distress or problems functioning, and lasts over time (American Psychiatric Association, 2013). Typically, a personality disorder develops in the late teens or early twenties and lasts throughout the lifetime.

Most of the social media craze focuses on the term and idea of "narcissist." While it is true narcissists can cause incredible damage in their relationships, there are also other diagnoses that can cause similar, if not worse harm. Narcissism falls into what we call the "cluster B" group of personality disorders, which includes Narcissistic (NPD), Antisocial (ASPD), and Borderline (BPD) Personality Disorders. Psychopathy is another dangerous disorder which also shares some traits with NPD and ASPD, yet it has a unique set of characteristics, so it is not included in the cluster B group.

While it may seem unnecessary for the public to understand these diagnoses, I believe it is crucial to gain awareness of these types who lack a conscience and empathy if you want to protect yourself from harm in your relationships. For the purposes of this book, we will mainly focus on NPD, ASPD, and psychopathy as the main pathological personality disorders that cause harm in relationships.

According to the *Diagnostic Statistical Manual of Mental Disorders (DSM-5)*, the prevalence in the general population for antisocial personality disorder is estimated at 3.3 percent, 6 percent for narcissistic personality disorder, and 4.5 percent for psychopathy (Sanz-García, Gesteira, Sanz, and García-Vera, 2021). **This means that approximately one out of every ten people in the United States lack empathy or a conscience.** In the book, *Women Who Love Psychopaths, Inside the Relationships of Inevitable Harm with Psychopaths, Sociopaths & Narcissists*, they estimate that 60–100 million people will be affected by these conscience lacking personality disorders.

The challenge in diagnosing these disorders is that psychopaths, narcissists, and sociopaths can be quite skilled at hiding their pathological behavior, even with highly trained mental health professionals. One can easily surmise that someone in a prison with a pattern of empathy lacking behavior could likely be diagnosed as a narcissist or psychopath. However, it can be challenging to identify a high functioning CEO who looks like a law-abiding citizen as someone with a similar empathy and conscience lacking psychological profile. I imagine we are grossly underestimating how many people actually have a disorder of low conscience or empathy for this reason.

PATHOLOGICAL LOVE RELATIONSHIPS

Ideally, our intimate relationships should be our safe haven, yet an astonishing "average of twenty-four people per minute are victims of rape, physical violence or stalking by an intimate partner in the United States, which is more than 12 million women and men over the course of a single year. Nearly half of all women and men have experienced psychological aggression by an intimate partner in their lifetime. Of this group, women ages 18 to 34 experience the highest rates of intimate partner violence. From 1994 to 2010, approximately 4 in 5 victims of intimate partner violence were female" (Black et al., 2010). Research indicates the main causes of intimate partner violence include substance abuse, extreme poverty, depression, anxiety, panic disorder, and personality disorders, and in particular, antisocial and borderline personality disorder (Ronggin et al., 2019).

When I contemplated the subtitle of this book, I wanted the public to easily understand it's focus, by choosing commonly used terminology to describe relationships with toxic, abusive partners, such as *narcissistic abuse, toxic relationships, domestic violence, intimate partner violence,* or even *love addiction.* Unfortunately, there is a significant lack of research, training, and awareness among the public and in the mental health field about these types of relationships, so we continue to use terms that are trendy, yet lack an accurate clinical description of this problem.

For the purposes of this book, we'll be exploring a specific type of intimate partner violence which we call "pathological love relationships," or PLRs, which was coined by Sandra L. Brown, MA, and The Institute for Relational Harm Reduction

& Public Pathology Education. According to Brown, a PLR describes a relationship where one partner has personality "pathology," such as narcissism, sociopathy, or psychopathy, and because of such pathology, the relationship will lead to "inevitable harm" to the non-pathological partner (Brown, 2009). This term is all-encompassing, as it addresses the fact that most pathological people typically do not have just one personality disorder but will often have traits of several of the cluster B types as we described earlier. While I may use the terms "narcissist" or "psychopath" throughout the book, it is important to note these personality types fit within the umbrella term of pathological love relationships. Furthermore, pathological love relationships are also considered intimate partner violence.

Fortunately, there is an incredible amount of insightful information in our world today about the topic of "narcissistic abuse." You can Google it, watch endless hours of YouTube videos, and work with therapists and coaches around the globe to help you recover. Most content is focused on helping you identify whether you are dealing with a narcissist, and how to heal. Questions like, *are you being gaslighted? Did he discard you? Is she love-bombing you?* All are typical strategies to help you identify if you are dealing with a narcissist. Many also talk about the connection between empaths and narcissists, through a spiritual lens. Suggestions to set boundaries, strengthen your self-worth, and strategies to help you leave are abundant.

The current therapeutic paradigm suggests that people who get involved with narcissists suffer from codependency, or even borderline or dependent personality disorder. However, there is such an astounding lack of research on these types of relationships that this becomes largely anecdotal information. It is formed by the tunnel vision of clinical experience vs. an abundance of research to confirm what we believe we see as clinicians.

The concept of codependency has its roots in the field of addiction, and usually describes a person who lacks a solid sense of self, lacks boundaries, and often enables the addict or abuser. While I completely agree that many victims experience codependent patterns, it simply doesn't explain the depth and complexity of these relationships, nor does it apply to the majority of survivors, as you'll soon learn. Furthermore, there are subtle levels of victim blaming in this concept that place too much responsibility on a victim to end this abuse. Quite simply, abuse is abuse, no matter how "codependent" you may be. Pathological people prey on others and can manipulate the most insightful, savvy, and boundaried people. Yes, a survivor must take responsibility for their healing, and we must use caution with this stigmatizing approach.

Sandra L. Brown, MA, and a team at Purdue University have taken the first steps in understanding what makes survivors so vulnerable to PLRs. In a 2014 study, they identified 63 percent of women survivors of PLRs did not have traits of codependency, nor did they have significant backgrounds of trauma. Instead, they had personality "super traits," which we will explore in depth in later chapters, which made them vulnerable to this abuse (Brown and Young, 2009). This groundbreaking study challenges the current paradigm and treatment model that weigh so heavily on seeing early trauma and codependency as the reason for a survivor's involvement in a PLR.

What is important to note about this is codependent patterns can be changed and healed, whereas personality traits are hardwired and usually can only be understood and managed. If the majority of therapists and coaches are trying to help survivors heal by addressing non-existent codependent patterns when the challenge lies within the personality, it will likely slow or prevent full and effective healing. As treatment providers, it is crucial for us to know the difference if we are to effectively help survivors. If you are a survivor, it is also extremely important to discern the differences as well so that you are not spinning your wheels in your healing journey. This book will help you understand and identify which patterns make you vulnerable.

INFLUENCES OF TRAUMA AND ATTACHMENT
Brown and Young astonishingly estimate that approximately 90 percent of survivors of pathological love relationships experience some form of trauma symptoms, and 50–75 percent develop diagnosable posttraumatic stress disorder (PTSD) or complex PTSD (Brown and Young, 2009). PTSD can include symptoms of sleep disruption, heightened anxiety and arousal in the stress response system of the body, depression, flashbacks or intrusive thoughts of traumatic memories, and other debilitating symptoms. Furthermore, there is growing evidence to show the connection between chronic health issues and disease to ongoing stress or trauma in a person's life.

Brown has identified one of the "hallmark symptoms" seen in survivors is intense cognitive dissonance, which essentially means a person is experiencing two conflicting thoughts, beliefs, or values in their mind simultaneously, which creates an internal state of anxiety and conflict. Most survivors experience this as confusing thoughts such as, "I love him/I fear him," or "I can't stand to be away from her/I can't stand to be with her" (Brown and Young, 2009). Like an exhausting internal game of tug-of-war, this dynamic strengthens and can destroy a survivor's sense of self-worth. They begin to feel confusion and shame around their decision to remain with a pathological partner despite the abusive behavior they endure. We will explore this dynamic in depth later in this book.

Brown also identified that PTSD looks different in survivors of PLRs, which leads many mental health professionals, as well as survivors, to miss or dismiss the severity of symptoms and impact that these damaging relationships can have on a person. Furthermore, there are many well-meaning coaches who have no clinical training or experience in working with trauma who have become self-proclaimed "experts" in helping survivors of narcissistic abuse. While much of their information can provide validation and support to survivors, without the trauma-informed background that is specific to PLRs, it can leave many survivors caught in an endless cycle of suffering from unhealed trauma, which also makes them vulnerable to returning to a PLR.

While there is still a need for more research in this ever-evolving field, I believe there can be deeper influences of trauma and attachment theory that significantly influence whether someone will fall prey to these relationships, or find themselves unable to clearly identify the danger they may be experiencing. It is crucial for us to continue to research, explore, and create a trauma-informed understanding of the dynamics of these toxic relationships. I am determined to increase our understanding of this dynamic so we can prevent and end these relationships before we have the "hindsight is 20/20" moment of regret.

It has only been in the last couple of decades we have truly begun to understand the impact and complexities of trauma on the body. Trailblazers in this area such as Dr. Peter Levine and Dr. Bessel van der Kolk have shifted the talk therapy paradigm and helped us understand that trauma is actually a physical experience, and in order to fully heal, we must involve the body in treatment. Talk therapy, while helpful, is like putting a band-aid on a gaping, infected wound. It might contain the bleeding, but it won't heal the infection. Any treatment with a survivor of a PLR who is experiencing symptoms of trauma must involve a focus on the body and nervous system for effective healing to occur.

As a therapist for almost thirty years, I've specialized in working with trauma, attachment and relationship trauma, and holistic approaches to mental health. I have worked with countless clients who have been abused by a pathological parent, friend, boss, or partner. I have also survived more than one pathological love relationship. In this book, I will share not only my personal and clinical experiences, but the cutting-edge research from experts in the fields of trauma, attachment, neuroscience, and pathological love relationships.

HOW TO USE THIS BOOK

You will find a mix of personal and clinical experience in this book. Some of my client stories are anecdotal, based on thirty years of experience with survivors. Others are stories from survivors I interviewed for this book but have changed names and identifying information. I have also intentionally changed the names and identifying information of my former partners to protect their identities.

This book is divided into three main sections, which will include a focus on external red flags, internal red flags, and strategies to strengthen your ability to identify and act upon red flags. In the first section, you're going to learn about pathology and how to spot the external red flags that you can identify in a partner (and this can also apply to others, such as a friend, family member, or boss). It will also include some of the common relational dynamics that occur in pathological love relationships. This is an important aspect of learning to protect yourself, as awareness is empowerment.

The second section, and most important message in this book, is focused on identifying your internal red flags. I am going to help you develop a unique language of insight and intuition that can help you navigate your way through any toxic relationship. We are going to learn about the language of trauma and how it manifests in your body, your health, and your relationships. We'll learn about the amazingly sophisticated connection between the mind and body, which is more accurate than any therapist, coach, book, or YouTube guru when understood and utilized properly. The truth is, you have all of the answers within you. The problem is, most people don't know how to understand the warning signs of our bodies and intuition, let alone know how to trust and act upon these messages. *You are your own expert.*

This brings us to the last section, where I'll share my LISTEN method to help you put your newfound knowledge into action so you can learn to identify red flags, trust them, and ultimately learn to protect yourself. You will hone your internal radar system so you can spot an unhealthy relationship before you become too involved. It will also improve your clarity if you are wondering whether you should exit a relationship.

If you are a therapist, coach, or other professional who is wanting to increase your understanding and ability to help others heal from pathological love relationships, this book will provide you with new insight and a trauma-informed lens from which to view this insidious form of abuse. This book may challenge many of the outdated and under-researched concepts you've learned about "narcissistic abuse," including a dismantling of the idea of codependency and love addiction as the main explanations for a person's involvement in these relationships. Instead, it will offer you a deeper understanding of pathological love relationships and the influences of trauma, attachment, and personality on the survivor's experiences.

So, what if I told you that you had the perfect tool to help you know if a partner was lying, betraying, or manipulating you? What if I told you that this tool was free, and available for you to use at this very moment? Or that this tool was the best radar, lie, bullshit, and narcissist and psychopath detector there is?

If this sounds enticing, then keep reading. This book is for you if you have ever been hurt by someone who has manipulated, abused, or lied to you. It's definitely for you if you've felt like you've lost yourself in a relationship. You may suspect or even know your partner is a narcissist or sociopath, or you may have no idea your partner has a personality disorder, but you are clear that something is wrong. If you have had a pattern of attracting relationships like this in your life, this book will help you reflect on this pattern and help you break free of this abuse. If you are currently in a relationship with an abusive partner, this book will help you trust your instincts, and find the strength and courage to leave. If you feel shame, confusion, low self-worth or self-esteem because of a relationship like this, this book will help you find compassion and acceptance for yourself, and a newfound trust in your innate wisdom.

PART ONE

EXTERNAL RED FLAGS: UNDERSTANDING PATHOLOGY

CHAPTER 1

RED FLAGS

Isabel sat across from me as she curled her legs up onto the couch, staring out the window of my therapy office. She was forty-eight years old and had been married for fifteen years to her husband, Darren. She grew up in a Catholic home as the youngest of five children. With emotionally distant parents, she had one protective older brother who shielded her from emotional and physical abuse by her other siblings. "I felt invisible. My dad was never home, and my mom was checked out. Now I realize she was probably very depressed and overwhelmed, but as a kid I felt ignored. My brother was the closest thing to a parent that I had, however he was a kid too."

Isabel wiped away her tears as she described the intense love she felt for Darren when they first met. "He was... He *is* my soul mate. We were so perfect for each other in every way. I had never met someone who was as passionate about politics, travel, and the outdoors as me. He had a lot of childhood trauma like me, so we understood each other. I felt so safe and loved. He was always there for me and because we had so much in common, it felt easy. When I was a child, I never felt loved like this. Even after I lost my job, he told me to stay home so I could pursue my passion of writing." She hadn't had a job in ten years and was completely financially dependent on him.

"But something changed after we got married. It's like he's two different people. Sometimes he is so loving, and he showers me with affection. Then other times he goes into a rage over the smallest comment or if I leave a dirty dish in the sink. He tells me I'm fat and is always forcing me to exercise with him. The worst part is that he sometimes stays out all night but when I get upset, he freaks out and calls me jealous and insecure. I'm so exhausted. I never know who I'm going to get," she sighed as she stared at the floor with a defeated look on her face.

She looked at me with an expressionless face, "I know he likes strip clubs. You know how men are. I figured if I let him have his freedom to just look at other women, he wouldn't be tempted to stray." She frequently discovered large sums of cash missing from their bank account, yet he told her it was none of her business since she didn't earn any of their money. She found nude pictures and sexually explicit conversations on his phone countless times, and even found women's underwear in the backseat of their car. Somehow, Isabel always managed to dismiss these suspicious events and seemed paralyzed by indecision about the relationship.

"I feel so stuck. I cannot imagine life without him. He's had so much trauma. If he could get into therapy, I think he'd really be able to change, but he tells me I'm the one that needs therapy and refuses to go. Sometimes I can't imagine staying with him. He's horrible. But I don't even know how I'd leave because I have no money," she shared as she looked at me with despair in her eyes. Isabel had been experiencing this dilemma for fifteen years.

THE FROG IN THE SAUCEPAN
Have you ever heard the story about the frog in the saucepan? The urban legend goes something like this: If you put a frog in a saucepan of water and slowly turn up the heat, it will remain in the water until it boils and dies. However, if you put the frog in the saucepan when the water is already boiling, it will immediately jump out to save itself. Now, I don't particularly like this story because I feel bad for the poor little frog, but the metaphor is useful, as it speaks to the phenomenon of how people lack the ability or willpower to react to danger that grows gradually. When in a relationship with a narcissistic or toxic person, we may be oblivious to the red flags until we've found ourselves in the pot of boiling water. Like Isabel, once you realize the pot is boiling, you are deep in the water and feeling excruciating pain. This is why we must improve our ability to see the red flags early in the relationship.

In an ideal world, we would be able to trust that all people are kind and safe and have our best intentions in mind. Unfortunately, that is not the world we live in. We are forced to become better detectives as we navigate relationships so we can surround ourselves with healthy, safe, and loving people. Usually when we look for red flags, we tend to look outside of ourselves, sizing up the characteristics of another person. We assess every potential partner, friend, colleague, and boss. We focus on all the things that make a person desirable or undesirable, from the clothes they wear, to their job or lifestyle, to their bank account, hobbies, and values. We look at their personality. Are they kind? Smart? Loving? Passionate? Rude? Self-centered? Angry? If you're a self-help addict or therapist, you might add an extra layer of trying to diagnose them.

One might think that most of us agree that there are basic necessities for a healthy, safe relationship. However, you'd be amazed to know just how subjective the list of red flags is for people. As a therapist, I've been astonished by things people don't consider red flags. Isabel's story is a case in point. I cannot make a list long enough to encompass the individual preferences for everyone. Furthermore, one of the most important lessons I want you to learn in this book is that no checklist, therapist, friend, or internet search is as valuable as learning to trust yourself. The problem is we have learned to doubt ourselves and usually this message came long before your relationship with a manipulative, charming narcissist or psychopath.

It is incredibly common to hear people say, "I didn't trust my gut," or "I had a feeling but…" This raises many questions for me. Why don't we trust and act upon these red flags? Why are red flags so clear to some people, yet invisible to others? And why is it that some people, even after being hurt in one abusive relationship, will go on to find another abusive partner, repeatedly missing and dismissing red flags?

It isn't uncommon to see a person who has been in a series of abusive relationships with a lifelong pattern of dismissing red flags. When you've done this consistently over time, you create a pattern of doubting yourself and the very signals that could steer you away from danger. To better answer these questions, let's start with increasing our awareness of the concept of red flags and the different systems we have at our disposal to help us assess for dangerous or toxic people.

THE LANGUAGE OF RED FLAGS

The 2021 Merriam-Webster Dictionary defines a red flag as a warning signal or sign, or something that indicates or draws attention to a problem, danger, or irregularity. This is what we are here to identify: the warning signs of a toxic or abusive partner. We use this term loosely in our culture, but let's start with a clear definition of internal red flags by discerning between gut feelings and intuition.

GUT FEELINGS

We often say things like "I have a gut feeling" or "trust your gut." Some people are more attuned to their gut signals, yet others may not realize the sensations they feel in their body are actual physical red flags that are alerting them to danger. The truth is, our gut is always speaking to us, but many of us don't know how to translate the sensations into meaningful messages, let alone trust these messages. We will learn in a later chapter about the gut-brain connection which actually gives some credence to this concept of gut feelings. Essentially, our emotional experiences can lead to gastrointestinal distress, reactions, or sensations and vice-versa, our gut reactions and sensations can lead to emotional experiences. Some examples include:

- a knot in the pit of your stomach
- sweaty hands

- tension or tightness in the body
- goosebumps
- nausea
- "butterflies" in the stomach
- feelings of peace, safety, or happiness after a decision is made
- diarrhea

INTUITION

Intuition is "the power or faculty of attaining to direct knowledge or cognition without evident rational thought and inference" (Merriam-Webster, 2021). We use the terms "gut feeling" or "I have a feeling" to describe what is usually an intuitive message, or a deeper level of knowing. From my research, it doesn't seem like there is one perfect explanation to describe intuition and how it works. There are both scientific, physiological explanations, and spiritual or energetic based explanations. We clearly still have a lot to learn. Scientifically, we can examine the incredibly powerful and still largely understood mechanisms of the brain. Some hypothesize intuition may simply be a series of lightning-fast processes that are reading every environment, situation, and person we encounter and filtering out any irrelevant details. Once filtered, our mind is sent an intuitive signal, such as *leave now, don't trust that person, don't get on that plane*. If we notice the signal, we have a choice to listen and act upon the signal or to ignore it.

A team of researchers from the University of New South Wales recently identified a technique that led to growing confirmation that intuition is actually a neurological process. The study exposed participants to emotional images outside of their conscious awareness, while asking the participants to make accurate decisions. This demonstrated that even when people were unaware of the images they were seeing, they could still accurately and confidently make decisions based on the content of the images. The simplified idea of this study is that our brains are actually taking into account information from past experiences, the current environment or situation, and using that information to predict future experiences, which we then weave into our decision-making because it feels like a "gut feeling" (Lufityanto, Donkin, Pearson, 2016).

Dr. Judith Orloff MD, Assistant Clinical Professor of Psychiatry at UCLA and author of *The Empath's Survival Guide: Life Strategies for Sensitive People,* shares that intuition operates in the right side of our brain, which connects through the brain's hippocampus, and then to our gut. Interestingly, women have a thicker corpus collosum, a connective portion of white matter that connects the left and right hemispheres of the brain. This means women tend to have better and faster abilities to access both hemispheres of their brains, allowing them to more easily integrate emotion, gut feelings, and the analytical, rational side of their brains into their decision-making processes. Essentially, women's brains are much more capable of making intuitive, yet rationally sound decisions. Since men's brains have a less developed corpus collosum, they tend to compartmentalize their thinking and can't move between logic and intuition as easily as women (Orloff, 2017).

This information is fascinating, especially when you consider the fact that more women than men become victims to pathological love relationships. It raises the question:

if women have a heightened ability to make intuitive and rationally sound decisions, why are they the majority that is falling prey to these relationships? The answer to this is likely complex. However, as we'll learn later, one piece of this puzzle may be contained in the fact that trauma can significantly impair the intuitive lines of communication within.

THE CLAIRS

If you consider yourself a psychic, empath, or intuitive, you may consider intuition as an energetic, psychic, or spiritual phenomenon. From this perspective, the language used to explain different types of intuitive messages is called the "clairs." The clairs are psychic abilities that can give us information through our senses. If you learn how to listen to your intuitive messages, you may notice that you experience them through one or more senses. Everyone has access to all of these clairs, but most of us are not tuned in to our intuitive abilities enough to recognize what they are. The clairs include the following:

- **Clairvoyance**–which is clear seeing. People who experience this may get visions in their mind's eye, which can seem like a daydream or image.
- **Claircognizance**–clear knowing. This is when we just "know" something, especially when we have no proof or information that would help us know it. These can include premonitions or warnings of future events.
- **Clairaudience**–clear hearing. This is when you hear words, sounds, or maybe even music in your mind's voice. This is different from "hearing voices" as an auditory hallucination which often have a persistent critical or persecutory nature.

- **Clairsentience**–clear feeling. This happens when a person can feel another person's emotions or pain in their own body. You may notice this if you are in a great mood and walk into a room with a depressed person, and then feel depressed too.
- **Clairalience**–clear smelling. This happens when you can smell odors that have no detectible physical source.
- **Clairgustence**–clear tasting. Much like clairalience, this is the ability to taste something that isn't actually there.

No matter how you define your warning signs, the key is to become an expert in identifying your unique red flag language so you can use it to your advantage. When I was with one of my narcissistic partners, despite being a couple of years into our relationship and planning a future together, I couldn't shake the nagging, intuitive feeling that told me we would not be growing old together. I consider myself a fairly intuitive person, and can often discern between intuition, wishful thinking and anxiety, yet this ability was compromised in a relationship with a pathological partner. My heart loved him. My brain embellished the fantasy of our lives together. Nevertheless, my intuition was serving up a platter of black nothingness when I tried to peer into our lives as a happy, loving retired couple making our way to the end of our lives together.

Had I truly been acknowledging the red flags while paying attention to my intuition, that could have ended the relationship sooner rather than later and spared myself some heartbreak. Instead, my mind tried to make up stories like maybe one of us dies early, or the world has an apocalyptic meltdown, and we all die together. You know what wasn't in my story? *Maybe he's an abusive narcissist and this relationship is doomed, Chelli.* That story only became clear once I realized in my frog in the saucepan moment, that he was actually not Prince Charming, but was instead, Prince Harming.

Now this is a good example of how we can get an intuitive message that gives us some information, but we may not necessarily know how to interpret it. In my case, this message didn't feel like a warning sign. It felt like information, like it was a fact. *You will not have a long future with this man.* The problem was that there was a disconnect between this information and what was happening in my relationship, and my brain, riddled with trauma, was interpreting the signs inaccurately.

INTERNAL VS. EXTERNAL RED FLAGS
We must learn to trust ourselves. We give away our power by asking friends and Google to validate our concerns about whether someone is harming us. (Side note: if you are asking Google or a friend this question, the answer is most often a "yes"). Remember, you do not have to become an expert at knowing whether someone is narcissistic or pathological. It is not your job to diagnose them or yourself. That is a job for a therapist. Yes, increasing your awareness of suspicious traits or behaviors in someone is a crucial step in learning how to protect yourself, but is just that, a step. I am going to teach you how to look for two types of red flags, both external and internal.

Let's start with external red flags, which are the behaviors, language, traits, and other things you witness in another person. This is where learning the characteristics of narcissists, sociopaths, psychopaths, and concepts like gaslighting and love-bombing is particularly helpful. You can Google this to death and find out all you want to know about pathological personalities. If you are truly suspicious about someone, follow your instincts and check out external and internal red flags. You can pay attention to whether they have friends, or a solid job history. Do a background check. In other words, check under the hood before you buy the car.

The problem is many pathological people can look incredibly put together on the surface. Jeffrey Epstein and Harvey Weinstein are perfect examples of this. Both were highly successful men who seemed to "have it all," yet were eventually found to be dangerous predators who got away with years of sexually assaulting women while surrounded by others who knowingly or unknowingly enabled their behavior. Many of the women who were lured in by these men shared their stories about initially being intrigued or excited to be near someone of their status, but later experienced gut feelings that something was wrong (internal red flag) once they were in a compromising situation with the predator (in a private room, for example), and then found it too threatening to leave or protect themselves. While most of us aren't dealing with Jeffrey Epsteins or Harvey Weinsteins, it is a good example of how simply looking for external red flags is not a reliable practice to help you truly discern whether someone is safe.

Here is the reality about red flags:

- We have ALL of the information we need to inform us of whether a person is safe and healthy *within* ourselves.

- Red flags are almost always present early in the relationship, but we usually miss or dismiss them.
- Therefore, while it is important to look for the red flags in the other person, we MUST learn to listen, trust, and act upon our own red flags, as they are more accurate and reliable than sizing up another person's behavior.

WHY WE MISS THE RED FLAGS

When dealing with charismatic, manipulative, pathological people, it can sometimes be difficult to see or accept even the most gigantic, glaring red flags in front of you. There are plenty of easily identifiable toxic people who wear it on their sleeves. Yet, there are even more who deceivingly "look good on paper." They could be the CEO of a major company or your beloved pastor at church. They could be preaching about love, kindness, and empathy to thousands of loyal followers. They could seem like the most sensitive, supportive, loving soul mate you've dreamed of your entire life. No matter how good they may seem, there are almost ALWAYS red flags in the beginning of every relationship, yet there are a few reasons why we miss them:

1. **We have personality "super traits" of agreeableness and conscientiousness.**

   In her book, *Women Who Love Psychopaths: Inside the Relationships of inevitable Harm with Psychopaths, Sociopaths & Narcissists* (2018), Sandra L. Brown, MA, shared extensive research to help identify what makes us vulnerable to psychopaths and personality disordered individuals. Brown's work challenges many commonly held misperceptions about people who experience what she terms "pathological love relationships," including the idea that many victims are codependent or have histories of trauma. Brown found over 60 percent of women who had experienced a pathological love relationship had two particular personality traits of agreeableness and conscientiousness. Personality traits are the fundamental essence of who we are and are generally with us for life. Essentially, these people are forgiving, trusting, compassionate, flexible, and generally see the good in others, which can draw them in to abusive relationships and keep them stuck.

2. **Red flags may present as positive traits or experiences early in a relationship and may only be identified in retrospect after a pattern of behavior has developed over time.**

This is very common, especially when dealing with narcissists, psychopaths, and sociopaths because of the mask they initially wear that hides the underlying toxic qualities. They can shower you with love and affection, appear incredibly charismatic and charming, and mirror everything about you so that you believe you've found your "One." This can also happen if you've experienced role modeling in your family or culture where oppressive, sexist, racist, or abusive behavior has been accepted and normalized. *If everyone else is doing it, then it must be acceptable, right?* Even therapists miss the red flags since they either lack the training or are also manipulated by the smoke screen, charisma, and charm of the pathological person. Most are also unaware of the unique presentation of a client who is experiencing relationship abuse. This is much like the example of the frog in the saucepan, where it is only in retrospect that you realize the red flags were there all along.

3. **We actively dismiss, deny, and dissociate from the red flags because of trauma or our attachment style.**

If you have survived a trauma in your past, have post-traumatic stress disorder (PTSD), or are experiencing symptoms of trauma while in an abusive relationship, your brain is likely engaging in many unconscious survival responses in an effort to keep you safe. Some of these responses include denial, repression of memories, and cognitive dissonance. Cognitive dissonance, which you'll learn about soon, is one of the most prominent symptoms of trauma resulting from a pathological love relationship. It is of particular concern, as it tends to keep people stuck in indecision about whether to stay or leave an abusive relationship. The brain can help us escape physical danger, but it also works hard to decrease our emotional pain by helping us avoid reminders of painful events. Living under the influence of trauma can significantly impact your ability to function, make clear decisions, and can dampen your awareness of the abuse you're experiencing.

Your attachment style, which you'll also learn about in a future chapter, can also impact your ability to accurately perceive and integrate red flag behavior in others, especially if you have what we call an anxious attachment, which can make you place the needs for connection above your own safety. Much like a personality trait, your attachment style has a pervasive, lifelong influence on how you live and love. Most people are unaware of the powerful influences of their attachment style on their relationships.

We often see red flags, but because of the three reasons mentioned above, we do nothing about the red flag that would truly protect us. We are too nice. We are too forgiving. We are in too much pain and denial. We are traumatized. We are too compassionate. Some of these prosocial personality traits are actually valued and helpful in life, however when you are dealing with pathology, they can be your greatest weakness. We'll explore these factors in the coming chapters as we begin to learn more about what makes us vulnerable, and how we can develop a better relationship with ourselves and our unique inner guidance systems.

CHAPTER 2

PATHOLOGY 101

Jonie sat in my therapy office, barely able to speak between her sobs. She had been out of state visiting her dying father for the last few weeks and had returned home to find a used condom in her bed and her jewelry boxes ransacked. One of her cherished diamond rings from her deceased mother was missing. Her husband Ricardo, to whom she'd been married to for twenty-five years, had stayed home while she was taking care of her father. Initially, she was stunned and confused about whether someone had broken into their home. It didn't take long for her to accept this discovery as the proverbial straw that would break the camel's back. She'd suspected her husband was cheating on her for years but couldn't admit to herself it was true.

She looked up at me with black mascara smeared beneath her eyes. "How did I not see this? How did I let this go on so long?"

I gently reminded her, "But you have seen this for years. You've been too traumatized to trust yourself." She sobbed again, feeling distraught, angry, and betrayed.

Jonie had been coming to therapy intermittently for the last year, but it had taken several months of therapy for her to share that Ricardo frequently went into rages, called her names, and was extremely controlling. She admitted she "lost it" at times when she felt angry or hurt by what she suspected was cheating, but she felt shame for her responses. Ricardo told her she had an anger problem and needed to get some help. She questioned why he kept all of his money in cash yet forced her to keep a tight budget only to be used for groceries or bills despite him being an attorney earning a high income. She found suspicious long hairs or cigarette ashes in the car (neither one of them smoked, and both had short hair), and often smelled perfume on him when he came home. He refused to talk to her when he was on business trips. When Jonie confronted him about these issues, his response was that she was a "controlling, jealous, gold-digger." He had a knack for turning the blame on her which made her question her reality.

When she first met Ricardo, she was mesmerized by his magnetic charm, intelligence, and wit. When he spoke, everyone listened. Jonie noticed he bragged about his accomplishments, but she thought, "he is really successful. How do you talk about your successes without making it seem like you're bragging?"

She vulnerably shared her insecurities with him in the beginning, fearing he wouldn't want a life with her because she "was only a preschool teacher" who was living paycheck to paycheck. Ricardo reassured her of his devotion, telling her that he'd had several "crazy ex-girlfriends," but he had never met someone like Jonie. He told her she was his soul mate, that he wanted to take care of her, insisting on paying for all of their dates, and buying her groceries and gifts. Ricardo's initial frequent contact with Jonie made her feel safe and cared for. She loved the attention.

The relationship moved quickly, and within two months, he asked her to move in with him. Jonie felt like she was living in a dream, yet within months of their wedding, Jonie began to see a new side of Ricardo. His once loving, affectionate demeanor would unexpectedly shift into anger and criticism. Sometimes she didn't understand what she had done to make him mad, but he always seemed to find something that upset him. She noticed he would frequently surprise her with a last-minute date if she had plans to see friends, expecting her to cancel. He seemed suspicious of her interactions with her coworkers and began to accuse her of cheating although Jonie denied this. He insisted on having access to her phone so he could monitor her. In the meantime, Jonie noticed him on his phone late at night, or sneaking out to their garage to make calls. When she asked who he was talking to, he'd bark at her "that's none of your business." Over the years, Jonie lost contact with most of her friends and family in order to appease Ricardo.

Many survivors of a pathological love relationship have a similar experience to Jonie's, which often have themes like this: The relationship begins with a dreamy connection, and the person sometimes seems like the perfect fit, or even too good to be true. The relationship tends to move fast, but the victim is often so enthralled with the partner that they simply believe it's acceptable to move fast since this person is so perfect. (I mean, what could go wrong when you have just met your soul mate?) Once the victim is connected or committed, the true personality is revealed, and the abuse begins. Many people will notice this quickly and leave, yet others may become trapped in lengthy, destructive relationships and for various reasons, find it impossible to leave. These relationships may be very brief or can last decades. These are telltale signs of a relationship with a "pathological" partner.

DEFINING PATHOLOGY

What does the word "pathological" mean to you? Unless you're a mental health professional, it may simply bring up images of serial killers and reruns of crime dramas on tv. Ricardo's behavior is one of many examples of pathology. According to the *DSM-5*, the term "pathology" describes certain behaviors, thoughts, and inner experiences that are atypical or unusual, distressful, dysfunctional, and even dangerous, as signs of a disorder. This includes:

- "significant disturbances in thoughts, feelings, and behaviors
- some kind of biological, psychological, or developmental dysfunction
- the disturbances lead to significant distress or disability in one's life
- disturbances do not reflect expected or culturally approved responses to certain events."

Pathology could include depression, anxiety and other common treatable mental health conditions, but it can also include disturbances in one's personality, which is generally difficult to manage and treat. Our personality traits are considered to be "hard wired," influencing every aspect of our lives which is why having personality pathology is so challenging. As we learned in the Introduction, personality disorders, and in particular, cluster B disorders, are the underlying cause of pathological love relationships. In order to understand these types of relationships, we first must understand personality pathology. This may seem like an overly clinical term to describe someone, yet there simply isn't a better word to describe the type of people who can wreak havoc on your heart and your life. It is incredibly important to know how to identify personality disorders as an external red flag so you can better protect yourself.

My goal here is not to turn you into a psychologist with the ability to diagnose every partner or friend you meet. However, many of us can be easily deceived into thinking that dangerous or pathological people are serial killers lurking in a van in a dark alley, or brazen criminals. People with personality pathology can be your grandfather, your yoga teacher, your priest, or your soul mate. Personality pathology knows no cultural, professional, socioeconomic, racial, religious, or gender boundaries, and can be found in people from all walks of life. As I shared in the Introduction, "narcissism" gets all of the attention and blame for what is actually a broader problem of pathology due to problematic personality traits and disorders that can cause harm in our relationships.

I'm going to arm you with information about psychopathy and narcissistic, borderline, and antisocial personality disorders as they are the underlying causes for pathological love relationships. Yet what matters more than getting a diagnosis correct is for you to know whether a person's behaviors are causing you distress or harm. This section is not meant to be the ultimate deciding factor in helping you identify whether your relationship is dangerous or detrimental to your health.

There are many stigmas associated with these disorders in the mental health field, yet my goal is not to increase this stigma. Every human being, even those who cause great harm to others, deserves compassion. Many of these disorders and traits have roots in childhood trauma and should be seen as such. However, the purpose of this book is to focus our understanding and compassion on the victims and survivors of pathological love relationships which are caused by partners with traits of personality disorders. This is a fact. These disorders are extremely challenging, if not dangerous at times, and they can be difficult to identify even for trained mental health professionals. It is therefore extremely important to educate you about this type of personality pathology, and the potential havoc it can wreak on your relationships.

Please note these cluster B disorders may overlap with each other, as a person may have several traits of one or more of these disorders. Also remember many of these disorders fall on a spectrum, where a person may have some of the traits, but are not fully diagnosable. This doesn't mean they can't do as much damage as someone with a full-blown diagnosis, however.

BORDERLINE PERSONALITY DISORDER
Borderline personality disorder (BPD) is one of the three cluster B disorders and can be a factor in a pathological love relationship. According the *DSM-5*, BPD "is a pervasive pattern of instability in interpersonal relationships, self-image,

and emotion, as well as marked impulsivity beginning by early adulthood and present in a variety of contexts, as indicated by five or more of the following:

- Chronic feelings of emptiness
- Emotional instability in reaction to day-to-day events (e.g., intense episodic sadness, irritability, or anxiety usually lasting a few hours and only rarely more than a few days)
- Frantic efforts to avoid real or imagined abandonment
- Identity disturbance with markedly or persistently unstable self-image or sense of self
- Impulsive behavior in at least two areas that are potentially self-damaging (e.g., spending, sex, substance abuse, reckless driving, binge eating)
- Inappropriate, intense anger or difficulty controlling anger (e.g., frequent displays of temper, constant anger, recurrent physical fights)
- Pattern of unstable and intense interpersonal relationships characterized by extremes between idealization and devaluation (also known as "splitting")
- Recurrent suicidal behavior, gestures, or threats, or self-harming behavior
- Transient, stress-related paranoid ideation or severe dissociative symptoms."

This disorder can lead to dramatic, high conflict relationship patterns. There has been considerable progress made in the field in developing effective coping and management strategies for people with BPD. Much like NPD, there are still questions about the exact cause of this disorder, but research points to several possible factors such as genetics, early childhood trauma or neglect, and structural differences in the brain, especially in areas that control impulses and emotion.

ANTISOCIAL PERSONALITY DISORDER AND PSYCHOPATHY

People often use the terms "sociopath" and "psychopath" interchangeably, as they share an overlap of characteristics. The *DSM-5* doesn't distinguish between the two, and only includes diagnostic criteria for antisocial personality disorder (ASPD), however, experts in the field identify a few differences. Someone with ASPD typically knows the difference between right and wrong but might rationalize or justify their antisocial behavior. They have low degrees of empathy and conscience. In contrast, a psychopath lacks empathy and has no conscience, typically not knowing the difference between right and wrong. Their illegal, criminal, or harmful behaviors tend to be pre-meditated, while a sociopath's behaviors can be more impulsive.

ASPD has also been shown to have environmental influences, such as early childhood neglect and trauma, whereas a psychopath can have distinct neurological, genetic, and biological influences. "Most psychopaths (with the exception of those who somehow manage to plow their way through life without coming into formal or prolonged contact with the criminal justice system) meet the criteria for ASPD, nonetheless most individuals with ASPD are not psychopaths" (Hare, 1996).

There is a misconception that someone who is "antisocial" is a person who doesn't like to socialize or is perhaps an introvert. However, this disorder has nothing to do with whether a person is socializing with others. The *DSM-5* uses the following criteria to identify someone with antisocial personality disorder, which is a person with a "persistent disregard for the rights of others, which is shown by the presence of three or more of the following criteria:

- Disregarding the law, indicated by repeatedly committing acts that are grounds for arrest
- Being deceitful, indicated by lying repeatedly, using aliases, or conning others for personal gain or pleasure
- Acting impulsively or not planning ahead
- Being easily provoked or aggressive, indicated by constantly getting into physical fights or assaulting others
- Recklessly disregarding their safety or the safety of others
- Consistently acting irresponsibly, indicated by quitting a job with no plans for another one or not paying bills
- Not feeling remorse, indicated by indifference to or rationalization of hurting or mistreating others
- These behaviors must have been present before age fifteen
- Antisocial personality disorder is diagnosed only in people eighteen years or older."

NARCISSISTIC PERSONALITY DISORDER

Due to the heightened awareness in the public psyche of narcissism, as well as it's common appearance in many PLRs, I am going to focus particular attention on this personality disorder. Narcissistic personality disorder is hardly a new concept, as it has roots in ancient Greek mythology. According to the myth, Narcissus was a proud, handsome man who stopped by a body of water and noticed his reflection for the first time. Upon seeing himself in the water, he became so enamored with his own reflection that he couldn't tear himself away, and he eventually died at the water's edge, gazing at himself. Indeed, narcissistic archetypes can be found in literature, media, and art that spans human history.

A common belief is narcissism is simply an extreme form of self-esteem. Psychologists have characterized narcissism as inflated, exaggerated, or excessive self-esteem, or even as "the dark side of high self-esteem" (Baumeister, Smart, and Boden, 1996). This concept would lead one to believe self-esteem can be measured on a spectrum, with narcissism at the high end. If this were accurate, there would be no narcissists with low self-esteem. However, research now shows narcissists can actually have high or low self-esteem, meaning self-esteem and narcissism are separate aspects of the personality. Narcissism is not simply a high amount of self-esteem (Brummelman, Crocker, and Bushman, 2016).

It is helpful to think of narcissism existing on a spectrum. The reality is that each and every one of us has narcissistic tendencies, but that doesn't make each of us a diagnosable narcissist. On one end of this spectrum, a healthy dose of narcissism may help us feel assertiveness, pride, and self-confidence. As you move further along the spectrum, the healthy ego can become self-centered and problematic, leading to a full-blown diagnosis of narcissistic personality disorder. The *DSM-5* indicates a person with NPD "possesses at least five of the following nine criteria, typically while lacking the actual qualities or accomplishments for which they demand respect and status:

- A grandiose sense of self-importance (e.g., exaggerating achievements and talents, expecting to be recognized as superior without commensurate achievements)

- Preoccupation with fantasies of unlimited success, power, brilliance, beauty, or ideal love
- Believing that they are 'special' and unique and can only be understood by, or should associate with, other special or high-status people (or institutions)
- Requiring excessive admiration and acknowledgement
- A sense of entitlement (unreasonable expectations of especially favorable treatment or automatic compliance with their expectations)
- Being interpersonally exploitative (taking advantage of others to achieve their own ends)
- Lacking empathy, unwilling to recognize or identify with the feelings and needs of others
- Often being envious of others or believing that others are envious of them
- Showing arrogant, haughty behaviors or attitudes

NPD usually develops in early adulthood or childhood. If a child or teen shows characteristics of the disorder, they cannot be diagnosed until age eighteen, as personality traits can change significantly in adolescence. If someone truly has NPD, the symptoms will be consistent in almost all social situations and will remain consistent over time, affecting most of their relationships (American Psychological Association, 2013). Not all narcissists look the same. We'll explore different presentations of NPD in the following chapter.

WHAT CAUSES NARCISSISM?
Current evidence suggests several possible origins of NPD, which are a combination of environmental, social, neurobiological, and genetic influences. Twin studies have identified a genetic component in NPD, as it can be passed down through

a family (Torgersen et al., 2002). Research also shows that narcissists have certain areas in the brain that are smaller which decreases the ability of the brain to perform in optimal ways, influencing its ability to process incoming information. Without this optimal functioning, the person experiences more antisocial and challenging behaviors (Kaya, Hanefi, and Murad, 2020).

Another study has associated the condition of NPD with a reduced volume of gray matter in the prefrontal cortex area of the brain, which is an area associated with compassion, empathy, thinking, and emotion. The results suggested that NPD may be related to a reduced or damaged capacity for empathy and emotional regulation, or the ability to manage emotions in healthy ways (Nenadic et al., 2015).

Along with these biological influences, social and environmental factors are still the biggest influences on the development of NPD. One significant influence is a child's dysfunctional attachment to a primary caregiver in early childhood. This can result in a child feeling insignificant and disconnected to family and community, leading to a belief they are unwanted and devalued as a person. Overindulgent and permissive parenting, or highly controlling parenting can also lead to the development of narcissism.

In *Gabbard's Treatments of Psychiatric Disorders*, the following factors are identified as promoting the development of narcissistic personality disorder:

- An oversensitive temperament (individual differences of behavior) at birth

- Excessive admiration that is never balanced with realistic criticism
- Excessive praise for good behaviors, or excessive criticism for bad behaviors in childhood
- Overindulgence and overvaluation by family or peers
- Being praised by adults for perceived exceptional physical appearance or abilities
- Trauma caused by psychological abuse, physical abuse or sexual abuse in childhood
- Unpredictable or unreliable parental caregiving
- Learning the behaviors of psychological manipulation from parents or peers

THE GOLDEN QUESTION: CAN THOSE WITH PERSONALITY DISORDERS CHANGE?

One of the most challenging aspects of cluster B disorders is that people who experience them are "ego-syntonic." This means they don't perceive their behavior is wrong or problematic for others, despite receiving feedback or consequences that says otherwise. When stressed, they will try to change the environment or people around them instead of themselves. Essentially, they believe their behavior is not the problem, instead, the "problem" is that someone has a problem with their behavior. Even if the behavior is illegal, harmful, or immoral, they will blame others and take no responsibility for their actions.

Conversely, "ego-dystonic" people will feel distress if they engage in behaviors, values, or ideas that are not aligned with who they believe they are as a person. When stressed, they will try to change themselves because they see their thoughts, feelings, or behaviors as problematic. For example, if you believe you are generally a hard-working person, but you find yourself spending too much time binge watching tv, you may beat yourself up a bit and decide to limit your time watching television. A person might say, "this isn't me, it's not who I am. I'm going to get off the couch and finish my work project" in response to a negative behavior they experienced.

Furthermore, narcissists believe that they are superior to others. Those with NPD, ASPD, and psychopaths also struggle to see the rules that apply to everyone else should also apply to them. This inability to self-reflect makes it very difficult for them to change, seek help, or integrate feedback from others about their challenging behaviors. It can be difficult for victims of a pathological love relationship to grasp how a narcissist or sociopath can think in this way, as it is so foreign to the way a person with an ego-dystonic personality, empathy, or any degree of self-reflection thinks. We want to believe they will feel empathy, or we can make them understand how their behavior hurts us. This often results in the victim begging, pleading, overexplaining, and often spending years waiting for them to "get it." It usually ends as a fruitless effort since the pathological person is largely incapable of seeing things the same way.

A person with a cluster B disorder who is ego-syntonic and believes they are superior to others will have very little motivation to change. They simply don't see what the rest of us see. They may be forced into therapy by the legal system or by a partner dragging them into couples therapy, but they tend not to seek help on their own. This is so important for you to understand, especially if you are clear that your partner is experiencing one of these disorders. If you are dealing with a partner with diagnosable or high degrees of a personality disorder, it is HIGHLY UNLIKELY they will see the need to change their behavior in order to save or improve your relationship.

In summary, these cluster B disorders can be extremely challenging and damaging. You may feel a great deal of compassion for a partner who experiences these traits, especially if they have a history of trauma. This is a good thing! We need more compassion for mental health issues in our world. However, having compassion should never equate to allowing yourself to be abused by someone who lacks a conscience or empathy. You can have compassion from a distance. These are serious mental health disorders and should be treated as such.

CHAPTER 3

THE FACES OF NARCISSISM

―

Felipe, a successful criminal defense attorney, is the top performer in his law firm. They love him for his endless success, yet they keep their distance, fearing the moment his mood shifts into his icy cold demeanor. He has a wide social circle and commands the attention in any social setting. He's funny, charming, witty, and engaging. He doesn't shy away from bragging about his success and has been known to criticize and belittle others in his presence. He skillfully turns every conversation back on himself, not seeming to offer much empathy or compassion for others. He has cheated on his wife with two paralegals in his firm.

Debrah is a quiet, introverted wife and mother who experiences low self-esteem and feelings of insecurity. She asks her family for reassurance when she feels slighted or criticized by her coworkers, which seems to happen daily. As a high school science teacher, she weaves her family's dinnertime conversations around scientific topics that only she understands.

When they share their confusion, she says "I'm surprised you don't know that. Everyone knows that!" She complains that everyone at school is jealous of her, as they don't recognize her level of intelligence. She rarely joins her husband and sons when they joke around unless it is to criticize them for making light of "serious situations." They have resorted to limiting their communication with her over the years to avoid upsetting her.

Samuel is pursuing his real estate career, however, has told his girlfriend he's had a series of misfortunes that have stalled his progress. She feels bad for him, allowing him to live with her after a month of dating, as he said he couldn't pay his rent. His social media account is full of bare-chested selfies. He tries to work at other jobs while building his real estate career but is usually fired within weeks. Of course, his dismissal is always someone else's fault. He has yet to help her with a single bill. He texts and calls her throughout the day and gets suspicious if she doesn't respond quickly, even if she's busy at work. She's noticed he creates dramatic fights or has a crisis whenever she has a big meeting or a night out with her girlfriends. She feels torn between meeting her obligations and taking care of his emotional needs.

Christian has spent many years in and out of prison for robbery, drug possession, and assault. When he is out of prison, he lives with his widowed grandmother who fears him, yet feels bad for him, as he lost both of his parents to drug overdoses at a young age. He often bullies her and steals her money, even though she barely survives on her disability checks. She fears he will hurt her if she makes him leave, so she allows him to come and go as he pleases.

Christian stole her wedding ring when she was asleep and pawned it for cash. He rationalizes this to his friends, saying it's "technically" his ring because he would inherit it when she dies.

Sara is a beloved yoga teacher who is kind, generous, and compassionate toward her students and fellow yogis. She is well-respected for her spiritual wisdom, leading thousands of students through yoga retreats and classes. Her partner, Camelia, has experienced Sara as needing constant attention at home. Sara perceives everything as criticism making Camelia feel like she isn't as "spiritually enlightened" as her. In response to Camelia's occasional anger and frustration with this behavior, Sara tells Camelia "you need to clean up your energy. I can't be around someone so negative." Camelia is confused, she sees Sara as two different people; loving, kind, and compassionate, but in the privacy of their home, she can be angry, aggressive, and defensive. Camelia's friends have a difficult time supporting her, as they struggle to imagine the rageful side of Sara she describes. She has started to believe she must need to do more "work" on herself so she can be more compassionate toward Sara. After all, she suffered a lot of trauma as a child, and she believes it must be the reason she can't make this relationship work.

HONING YOUR NARCISSIST RADAR
Each of these examples are presentations of narcissistic personality disorder. In the cases of Christian and Samuel, there are also traits of antisocial personality. Considering the complexities, variations, and public focus on narcissistic personality disorder, I decided NPD deserved its own chapter in this book. While the *DSM-5* only has one official diagnosis

for narcissism, there are some variations that have been made popular by mental health professionals and the internet. If you search "types of narcissism" on the internet, you will find an astonishing mix of headlines with results like "the seven types of narcissism," or "the three types of narcissism, etc." Some of these are backed by research, yet others are anecdotal, meaning they aren't necessarily clinically accurate or reliable. While the *DSM-5* traits that were identified in the previous chapter must be present to formally diagnose narcissism, some of these traits can be camouflaged by the early love-bombing, manipulation, and mirroring.

The bottom line is that narcissists can be extremely challenging to identify. As a therapist who has worked with this disorder for decades, I can often pick out a narcissist within minutes of an interaction, yet I have also missed red flags in others. Of course, this is exactly why I'm writing this book, so I can help us all become better at identifying them and protecting ourselves. While this has certainly made me question my abilities as a therapist at times, I know I am not alone. Not only have I interviewed many therapists who have fallen prey to narcissists in their personal lives, I've also heard countless stories of survivors who worked with therapists who didn't recognize this issue.

In fact, in most graduate training programs, therapists receive a very basic education about this complex disorder that can cause immense damage to its victims. This is noteworthy, as it is not uncommon for a well-meaning therapist to give inappropriate or even destructive advice to clients who are dealing with narcissistic partners. This often happens in couple's therapy, where one partner is a narcissist and may charm, lie, and manipulate the therapist into believing the victim is actually the problem.

I'm going to cover six common types of narcissistic presentations, but this list doesn't identify all of the subtypes that are discussed in media and literature.

THE GRANDIOSE NARCISSIST

When most people think of a narcissist, they think of what we call the grandiose or "overt" type. The grandiose narcissist (GN) most closely meets the standard *DSM-5* characteristics of this disorder. They tend to wear their narcissism on their sleeves. They have no shame in bragging about their real or imagined accomplishments, lack empathy, have a strong sense of entitlement and often a belief that rules are for everyone else except them. They may one-up, openly criticize, or belittle others. They love attention and may at times use flattery, charm, and charisma to draw others in. This is also called the "overt" type because their narcissism is outwardly displayed.

CHARACTERISTICS OF GRANDIOSE NARCISSISM:
- See themselves as superior to others
- May use charm or flattery to impress or attempt to connect with others
- Can appear arrogant, especially around others they feel superior to
- Expect special treatment and may believe they are above the law
- Have a sense of entitlement
- Try to attract attention to themselves in both negative and positive ways

- Often have fits of rage and anger which can escalate into violence
- Expect admiration and others to agree with them, and may express anger if they don't receive this
- Lack of empathy
- May ridicule or attack others to show their superiority
- Display a "Jekyll and Hyde" personality, alternating between charm, anger, or rage

A grandiose type also experiences *adaptive* or *maladaptive* narcissism. Adaptive grandiose narcissists, such as Felipe and Sara, build their self-esteem with ambitious health, career, or lifestyle goals that help protect their underlying insecurities. They may be persuasive, engaging, charismatic, and can be successful in leadership roles. These types may be CEOs or politicians who can have successful careers but will still have the underlying narcissistic qualities and can be exploitive and manipulative. The maladaptive type, such as Christian and Samuel, is not able to maintain successful roles, exerting power, manipulation, and control to achieve their goals. Grandiose traits tend to be related to substance abuse and often have an overlap of antisocial personality disorder traits (Russ, Shedler, Bradley, and Westen, 2008).

Narcissism is prevalent in the entertainment industry, CEOs, and in positions of leadership and power. However, it also affects your average Joe (or Jane), with no position of power or influence. Narcissists may be involved in careers, businesses, political offices, spiritual or religious groups, or charitable organizations that are aligned with generosity, charity, serving others, and promoting the well-being of others. This can be very deceiving, as most people assume a person in such a role must be doing it since they have empathy and truly care about others' well-being. Nonetheless, you must remember a narcissist's intentions are based on how they are perceived as a "good person" and not about doing good because they truly care about others. As we'll learn later on in this book, it is important to not make assumptions about a person based on their outward appearances. There are many wolves in sheep's clothing in the world.

THE COVERT/VULNERABLE NARCISSIST
The second, less known type of this disorder is vulnerable narcissism (VN), as we see in the example of Debrah. Many people interchangeably use the terms "covert" and "vulnerable" narcissist, but the correct clinical term is actually "vulnerable narcissist." Due to a lack of awareness about this subtype among the public and mental health professionals, along with its more subtle presentation, vulnerable narcissism can be particularly dangerous and easy to miss even by trained professionals.

Vulnerable narcissists are very preoccupied with fears of abandonment and rejection, experiencing envy and jealousy of others which may not be openly expressed. They are prone to depression, anxiety, self-harming behaviors and suicide attempts (Russ, Shedler, Bradley, and Westen, 2008). VN's tend to have extreme swings between feeling inferior and superior, depending on the situation in their daily lives. At their core, they fear they are worthless and shameful; they may even share these feelings with you, which can invoke your empathy and compassion. They tend to be very passive aggressive. What's most confusing is they can exhibit a side of themselves that is somewhat self-reflective, having themes of shame, weakness, and fear of what others think of them. This is very different from the grandiose narcissist who would never display this level of vulnerability.

CHARACTERISTICS OF COVERT/VULNERABLE NARCISSISM:
- Hypersensitive to perceived criticism
- Lack of empathy
- Defensiveness
- Often experience bouts of depression and anxiety
- Use subtle attempts to gain compliments and praise
- Presents themselves as the victim
- Seek out caretakers whom they can exploit
- Passive aggressive
- Blame others for their failures and circumstances (exes, institutions, their boss)
- May create drama or crises to seek attention
- May be financially controlling or drain others of money
- Can be insensitive and smug
- May create dramatic displays of emotion on cue
- May appear generous and caring in an effort to gain recognition
- Envious or jealous of others, but may not express this
- May seem self-deprecating or humble, yet this may be an attempt to gain praise or compliments
- Also display a "Jekyll and Hyde" personality

A vulnerable narcissist may seem withdrawn, shy, humble, and self-deprecating. People often feel sorry for them early in the relationship, as they have a knack for presenting themselves as a victim. Unlike the grandiose narcissist who might call their exes "crazy," the VN may take a different approach and talk about how their ex was unaffectionate, controlling, unsupportive, or even abusive. You may even hear elaborate stories of how this happened, in an attempt to have you believe they were mistreated.

The VN may actually appear to be concerned about how they appear to others, may admit they have low self-esteem, or seem humble in nature. They may even seem like the kind of person everyone loves, as a toned-down version of the grandiose narcissist. They don't outwardly brag about themselves but will skillfully downplay their accomplishments in order to receive praise. I once had a VN partner who would often talk about a friend or family member who was dealing with a hardship, and he would start the conversation off with something like, "My friend Andy is having a hard time right now. I know I helped him because I was able to give him a lot of good advice, and I could tell he really appreciated me. I think he is grateful to have me as a friend." Instead of sharing concern about Andy, the focus was on how amazing he was for helping Andy.

Another example is a smugness, or a belief they are superior to others. The GN might say something blatant like, "I'm the best employee in the business. I know more than my boss or anyone else will ever know." Whereas the VN is going to make more subtle comments that show they believe they are superior. My VN partner would often say, "I'm surprised you didn't know that," to many topics in conversation, especially ones he created that were highly intellectual and specialized, such as an obscure scientific fact. He never outright said he was better or smarter than me, but the message was "You're dumb, and I'm smarter than you!"

The GN may outwardly criticize, ridicule, or shame you for something, whereas the VN might gently approach you and explain why you are at fault, and they are not to blame. They may express their dismay with you by acting like a victim of your abuse, and end up making you feel crazy, confused, and horrible about yourself. You'll then be rewarded with passive aggressive insults later on to make sure you know that you made a mistake.

A relationship with a vulnerable narcissist can feel like "death by a thousand paper cuts," whereas abuse by a grandiose narcissist can feel like an outright blow, along with a thousand paper cuts. I have had the unfortunate experience with both types, and while both were equally destructive, they had distinct qualities to them. The VN was incredibly deceiving and more difficult to identify, whereas the GN was easier to identify early on in the relationship. It is important to know there are these two types so you have a better chance of identifying a narcissist.

THE MALIGNANT NARCISSIST

The most severe and dangerous type is the malignant narcissist who can be extremely malicious, manipulative, aggressive, and sadistic (takes pleasure in hurting others). This type has traits of both narcissism and antisocial personality disorder, meaning they lack a conscience and empathy, may engage in illegal, immoral, and dangerous behavior. They are motivated by seeing others in pain and have no empathy. Any attempts to outsmart them or fight back will likely fail.

CHARACTERISTICS OF THE MALIGNANT NARCISSIST:
- Paranoia, mistrust in others
- Takes pleasure in the pain of others

- May seek revenge against people who have criticized or wronged them
- Arrogant
- Complete lack of empathy, remorse, and regret
- Self-serving exploitative and manipulative behavior
- Have an extreme need for power
- Obsession with dominating others
- Highly aggressive

If you are with a malignant narcissist, it is extremely important to seek help, leave, and end all contact. They are extremely dangerous and challenging, due to their lack of empathy, need for revenge, and sadistic qualities. It is vital to seek help from professionals and even law enforcement in order to separate yourself safely.

THE SEXUAL NARCISSIST

A sexual narcissist will have the same general traits of NPD; however, their narcissistic behavior will be magnified in the context of sexual interactions and relationships than in other areas of their lives. Often, a sexual narcissist may cheat, engage in violent sexual encounters or sexual assault, and will use sex to manipulate others.

CHARACTERISTICS OF A SEXUAL NARCISSIST:
- Needs validation and praise for their sexual performance
- May use sex to pull you into a relationship
- Is focused on their own sexual needs, but not yours
- Will expect sex in return for favors or gifts
- Will brag about their sexual skills and abilities
- May react in anger, pouting, or putdowns when you refuse sex or don't offer enough praise

- May manipulate you into having sex, and lack empathy for this type of behavior
- Believe they are owed sex whenever they want, despite what you're doing at the time
- Feel perfectly willing to trick, deceive, or manipulate you into having sex
- Care little about what you want in bed
- May criticize you or make you feel bad for not performing in ways they desire

THE CEREBRAL NARCISSIST

The cerebral narcissist derives their self-importance from their intellect and will attempt to outsmart you. They love to show off their intelligence by speaking about highly intellectual topics, or areas in which they know you lack knowledge. They will attempt to make you feel unintelligent in both subtle and overt ways.

Characteristics of a cerebral narcissist:

- Constantly flaunting or improving their intelligence (the smarter they appear, the better they feel about themselves)
- A need to have the upper hand in discussions about certain topics, so they can show you that they know more than you
- Believe they should be in power positions because of their intelligence
- May only want to associate with people whom they believe to be intelligent, and look down upon everyone else
- Purposely uses words, jargon, or concepts that are beyond your level of knowledge

- May make smug or subtle comments to highlight the fact that they know more than you

You can't outsmart a cerebral narcissist. It is better to let them believe they are smarter, right, or better than you, than to engage in an argument. Most importantly, it is good to recognize this as narcissism, instead of allowing these manipulative tactics to make you feel unintelligent or less than your partner in any way.

THE SPIRITUAL NARCISSIST

A spiritual narcissist will use their spiritual practice to increase feelings of significance and power, rather than decrease their sense of importance or develop deepening humility. These types are particularly dangerous, as they may appear as the "wolf in sheep's clothing" when people are more vulnerable and trusting in spiritual or religious practices. They are commonly seen as leaders of religious or spiritual cults, who have manipulated and brainwashed followers. However, they can be anywhere and anyone, including Joe Schmo in your yoga class who is bragging about how enlightened he is.

CHARACTERISTICS OF A SPIRITUAL NARCISSIST:
- Striving to be a master of their religion/spiritual practice
- Belief that they are chosen or special
- Overemphasizing levels of mastery in spirituality
- Unforgiving and inflexible
- Don't walk their talk (preaches about loving everyone, yet condemns or ostracizes certain people)
- May manipulate you into doing things you're uncomfortable with, claiming God told them to guide you

I could create a long list of different ways that narcissism presents itself. If you take anything from this chapter, the most important piece is to understand the differences between grandiose and vulnerable narcissism, as the latter can be so difficult to spot. Do you need to become an expert at knowing all of these types so you can be a better detective? No. This is just a sampling of external red flags to help you sharpen your radar. However, there's a better way. We are going to learn more about what it takes to become a highly skilled narcissist and pathology detective, so stay with me here.

CHAPTER 4

MINDFUCKERY

One sunny spring day many years ago, I was dancing around my house to Michael Franti music, finding a rare moment of solitude. For a few hours, I relished the idea that I had no one to take care of, no one to feed, and no one to please. My kids were with their dad, and my partner was riding his bike in the mountains. I brushed off a moment of mom guilt that was nagging me to pick up the house, do the laundry, and *all the things*. I needed this time like I needed air.

Andrew texted me midday to let me know he would be a couple of hours late getting home from his bike ride. I was secretly giddy with excitement, cherishing the idea of a few more hours to recharge. I happily texted back "no worries at all, take all the time you need! I am happy to have some alone time," as I relaxed deeper into the unexpected gift of a day alone.

A few hours later, he silently walked in the door with a sheepish scowl on his face and said nothing as he plunked down in the corner of the couch, hunching his tall, muscular body into an awkward, angular hump. He hid his face in his hands, as if he was trying to curl six lanky feet of a grown man into a fetal position. I sat next to him, immediately reaching my arm across his back, fearing something horrible had occurred.

"Hey, what's going on?" I asked.

"I'm scared that you're going to take my bike away" he said in a tearful, boyish voice. I bristled as my body sensed danger before my mind recognized the threat. My eyebrows raised in confusion.

With trepidation I asked, "why would I take your bike away? You're an adult. I would never even consider that."

He whispered timidly, "because I was late. Please don't be mad at me." He cowered, hiding his head in his hands as if I was going to hit him. I scrunched my brow, and carefully held back my expression that wanted to say *what in the hell is going on here?*

I said in a soothing voice, trying to hide my confusion, "but I texted you that it was fine, and even asked you to take your time. I was actually happy to have more free time today. I'm not mad at all!"

He lifted his head from his hands and stood up, towering above me. There was a darkness in his eyes as I felt a building undercurrent of rage. He seethed "you ruined my afternoon. I couldn't even relax because I knew you'd take my bike away and be mad at me."

My head was spinning, and my body began to tremble as I found myself pleading my case, "but I told you it was ok and to take your time. Didn't you see my text? I really did want the free time. Do I seem angry with you?" His shoulders adjusted again, and straightened him into a towering giant, adding what seemed like another six inches to his intimidating presence above me. He looked me in the eyes, his face crooked, red, and vacant. This was no longer the man I thought was my soul mate...kind, gentle, and loving. This was someone new; someone dark and unfamiliar.

Suddenly the frightened, childlike voice disappeared, and he bellowed "why couldn't you just tell me to come home later? You ruined my entire afternoon! You don't have any respect for my need for nature and exercise. You always ruin it. You're just like my ex! I demand an apology!"

Holding back my tears, face to the ground, my mind whipped up a defense, but my mouth whispered "You're right. I am sorry." I waited for his acceptance that would signal the end of this battle, but he put his hands on his hips and rolled his eyes.

"Whatever, you're just mouthing the words. *I DEMAND A REAL APOLOGY.* Now WHAT are you sorry for?"

I swallowed everything in that moment as an act of solidarity with Safety. She trumped my truth, my integrity, my self-respect, my pride and led me out of a battle I was never going to win.

"I am truly sorry for ruining your day by expecting you home sooner. I should have been more clear. I know how important your time in nature and exercise is to you. I love you."

"Ok, thank you! I just need you to respect my needs!" he scoffed as he walked away. I stood shaking, nauseous, my mind replaying the conversation, still completely baffled by what had transpired. I ran through the scenario again and again, trying to find the moment that I upset him. *What had I done? Was I being controlling? Was it my tone? Had I told him I'd take his bike away before? Did I miss something?*

It was so absurdly crazy that part of me was clear that I needed to leave this man. Yet another part of me felt stunned and confused. I rehashed every text, every word, and even my body language to identify my part in this bizarre interaction. He attempted to make me feel guilty for something I never did, and it was clear to me at that moment that if I continued to resist, it would have fueled his rage, pouting, and criticism. Having encountered many bizarre moments like this over the last year or so, I had started to doubt my perception of reality. I was constantly googling narcissism (even though I knew this so well as a therapist) and sharing countless stories with my friends so I could trust what I was experiencing. I started journaling after every interaction so I could remember what happened, as I began to doubt myself, even in moments like this where it was clear that I was dealing with someone who was unstable and manipulative. My mind kept searching for proof of what my body and soul already knew. He was indeed a narcissist, and I had missed, and dismissed the red flags I encountered early in the relationship.

DYNAMICS OF PATHOLOGICAL LOVE RELATIONSHIPS

My story is not a particularly dangerous or violent example of narcissistic behavior compared to many I've heard or experienced over the years. However, it is a classic example of how a narcissist can manipulate experiences to shift the blame onto you, make you feel bad about yourself, or make you literally question your sanity. I'm going to highlight several dynamics and communication patterns you may experience in a pathological love relationship in this chapter, as we continue to identify the external red flags that can indicate your relationship is causing you harm.

After my personal experience along with countless client stories about the emotional turmoil, confusion, and despair of being in relationship with a narcissist, there was one word that encompassed the sensation of these abusive experiences, *mindfuckery*. Clearly, this is far from a professional term, but it is undoubtably what the experience feels like. Please forgive my divergence from the *DSM-5*, as I've never found a term to encompass this insanity written in its pages. All humor and f-bombs aside, let me be clear. Every single one of these dynamics are considered psychological, mental, or emotional abuse. Please read these with that in mind, so that if you are doubting yourself, you can begin to find clarity in the fact that you are being abused.

GASLIGHTING
The term "gaslighting" came from "Gas Light," a 1938 play in which a husband manipulates his wife in an attempt to make her feel insane so he can commit her to a psychiatric hospital and ultimately steal her inheritance (Thomas, 2018). Gaslighting is one of the most common and destructive forms of emotional and mental abuse in a PLR. This dynamic often occurs in both subtle and obvious ways, and over time, can make it challenging for a victim to identify or leave an abusive relationship as they may not even realize

it's happening. It can leave you second guessing yourself, your memory, and your perception of reality. The number one red flag to indicate you have experienced gaslighting is that you are left feeling dazed, confused, and wondering if something is wrong with you, or, *what in the hell just happened?*

Examples of gaslighting mindfuckery include:

- Lying and denial. "That never happened."
- Your memory is horrible, or their memory is horrible (as in, if they don't remember it, it never happened.)
- Minimizing your thoughts and feelings. "You're too sensitive, controlling, needy, etc."
- Telling you "You're crazy!"
- Discrediting you or your experience. "It wasn't that bad!" or "No, that's not how it happened!"
- "I'm sorry you have a problem with my anger" instead of "I'm sorry I hurt you when I was angry."
- Telling you that everyone else thinks you are crazy, controlling, etc.
- Blaming you for your reactions to their abuse. "You shouldn't have made me mad. It's your fault I am angry."
- Blame shifting in order to make you feel responsible for something they did.
- Using loving, compassionate responses to disarm you. "You know how much I love you. I would never hurt you."
- Repeatedly telling stories that have been twisted in their favor. For example, after pushing you into a wall, they begin retelling the story about the time you were so clumsy you fell and hit the wall, and you begin to question your perception of the event.

To apply this to my example, Andrew used gaslighting by coming into my house acting scared and fearful of me, despite the fact I had happily told him it was fine to enjoy his day out. Instead of coming in and saying, "sorry I'm late," or not saying anything at all since I told him he didn't need to come home early. He created a dramatic display of emotion, with the subtle message that I was abusive to him, and he should be afraid of my reaction. He then pushed me to apologize for something I didn't do. I was left feeling baffled and completely astonished at the bizarre interaction.

I can't write this chapter without calling attention to the gaslighting and denial that occurs to women on a societal level. We have seen this dynamic play out in politics, in corporations, and in high profile legal cases. A great example of the gaslighting of women survivors of sexual assault is often seen in cases with men who appear to have assaulted many women, as in the cases of Jeffrey Epstein and the US Women's national gymnastics team doctor, Larry Nassar. In both cases, several women came forth with similar reports of sexual assaults by these men, yet there was a pattern of doubting or dismissing these women altogether. If you pay attention to the verbiage used when describing the victims of Jeffrey Epstein, you see phrases such as "underage women," instead of "children, teens, or minors," or "sex with minors" instead of "rape". Survivors are treated like they are guilty of things they haven't done, or they are over-reacting. When women live in a world where their voices and experiences are silenced, minimized, and doubted, it leads to gaslighting of epic proportions.

LOVE-BOMBING

The term *love-bombing* appears to have been coined by members of Sun Myung Moon's Unification Church (a cult) in the seventies, stemming from the practice of showering new members with displays of warmth and attention to lure them into the group. This is a potent technique narcissists and other toxic people use to seduce you into the relationship or to manipulate you into forgiving and forgetting the harm they've done to you. Like any of these dynamics, it can be subtle or more obvious. Regardless, it can make you feel like you are loved, cherished, and desired by the narcissist.

Examples of love-bombing:

- Offering gifts, financial support, or experiences
- Proclaiming their love for you early (i.e., saying "I love you" within days or weeks of a new relationship)
- Showering you with affection and attention
- Wanting to be in constant contact with texting, phone calls, or time together
- Pushing gifts or experiences upon you without consideration of your needs or desires
- Promises of a future together, especially early in the relationship
- Make claims that you're their soul mate at the beginning of the relationship
- You may feel like you're being saved or rescued
- It feels too good to be true
- They put you on a pedestal

Love-bombing can feel intoxicating, especially in the beginning of a new relationship. In fact, this is probably one of the biggest early red flags to look for in a partner. Pathological partners can be quite skilled at showering you with so much attention and love that you may truly believe you've met your soul mate or perfect partner. A sign that you are being love-bombed is when you feel intoxicated by the relationship and find yourself moving fast, thinking this is too good to be true, or focusing all of your attention on the new partner. While a new relationship with a non-pathological partner can also leave you feeling excited and in a dreamy state, they will lack the constant need for connection and fast track to commitment of a PLR.

Another aspect of this form of mindfuckery is that after an abusive episode, the pathological person, and in particular, narcissists, will often love bomb you with apologies, gifts, attention, and promises of change, which seduce the victim back into the relationship. What adds fuel to the seduction fire is when a victim has the personality super traits of agreeableness and conscientiousness, responding to this dynamic with forgiveness, optimism, flexibility, empathy, and loyalty.

MIRRORING
In the beginning of the relationship, you may believe you've met your perfect match, as you find the pathological partner shares your interests, passions, behaviors, and even your gestures and mannerisms. Like with love-bombing, this magical feeling that you've met your perfect mate can lure you into the relationship rather quickly. Because it seems so perfect, you let down your guard. But the truth is, these types are simply skilled at noticing these details about you. They pretend to share your interests by *mirroring* them back to you. They do this because they lack a solid sense of identity, so they

look for it in others. Furthermore, they struggle to create true intimacy, so they reflect your desired level of intimacy back to you. Unfortunately, victims of PLRs usually find out later in the relationship that the narcissist doesn't actually share the same interests and may even criticize you or prevent you from engaging in them.

Examples of mirroring:

- Sharing the same interests as you, but seeming to lack a depth of knowledge or experience about them
- When you try to discuss a shared interest in detail, they change the subject or gaslight you
- You are unable to find examples or proof of them sharing the interest (i.e., he says he loves reading, but he can't name a book he's read, nor does he own any books)
- They don't walk their talk when it comes to these interests

SUPPLY

Narcissistic supply refers to the narcissist's need for constant admiration and attention. Using their charm and manipulation, they prey on vulnerable people to become this supply. You may experience their rage if you challenge their behavior or if they perceive you have somehow criticized them, as this cuts off their supply of admiration. If you break up with them, they will feel a need to rejuvenate their supply and may find a new relationship quickly after the breakup. They can never get enough of this. In a sense, it is a coping mechanism for them, as they are dependent on others to fill their empty sense of self. If you have ever felt completely drained by your partner, this is why. They are feeding off your attention and admiration.

PROJECTION

Projection is a defense mechanism that is prevalent in people with personality disorders and addiction, however we all tend to project at times. This dynamic occurs when a person identifies their negative thoughts, beliefs, or feelings in someone else in an effort to protect themselves from the discomfort of identifying these things as their own. An example is a cheating wife who accuses her loyal husband of cheating. Instead of addressing her guilt and shame, she begins to accuse him of something she is actually doing. It usually helps the person feel better about uncomfortable or unconscious thoughts, behaviors, or feelings. Projection is frequently used as an aspect of gaslighting.

WORD SALAD

Have you ever experienced a pattern of engaging in endless hours of conflict with a partner, and feeling so lost that you forget what even started the argument? You may be experiencing narcissistic word salad. The term "word salad" actually describes a communication pattern with unintelligible, disorganized speech that is usually seen in schizophrenia. However, the term has earned a place in narcissistic slang vocabulary to describe the confusing, crazy making communication patterns that occur with a narcissist. They are masters at creating drama and conflict and can turn the smallest topic into an endless argument, moving from one confusing topic to the next. You may feel like you're walking through a mine field, and as soon as you find a moment of resolution, they get triggered by the way you breathe or blink your eyes or bring up something from three weeks ago. They use circular reasoning, denial, blame shifting, lying, and misrepresentations of events to confuse you and avoid responsibility. When you try to understand or argue back with something that is rational or reasonable, you may be attacked for being the "irrational one." A word salad argument can span hours or even days and is utterly exhausting.

SMEAR CAMPAIGNS
Narcissists usually don't go down without a fight. They want to stay in control and must maintain their image at all costs. They are known to pull unwitting participants into the abuse by engaging in smear campaigns to discredit you. They will try to destroy your reputation, lie, or share vulnerable information about you to anyone who knows you, including your friends, family members, and even coworkers in an attempt to turn them against you. This is particularly common during a breakup or divorce and can be incredibly destructive. Because of the narcissist's charm and manipulation, many people will fall for their stories of being victimized by you, or about how concerned the narcissist is for your mental health since you seem so unstable. Other pathological people can engage in these campaigns as well.

FLYING MONKEYS
Remember the wicked witch in The Wizard of Oz, and her pack of flying monkeys who did her dirty work for her? This is where this term originated. As if the mindfuckery from one person wasn't enough, the charming, manipulative narcissist or pathological person will often seek help from others, a.k.a., their flying monkeys, to destroy you. This can be incredibly isolating and painful, as these people unwittingly side with the pathological person and

may even engage in putting you down, dismissing you, or gaslighting you because of the things the person has shared with them. They may act as a messenger for them, and can even become aggressive and threatening, depending on the person.

BANDWAGONING

Along these lines, the term *bandwagoning* refers to the pathological person's tendency to make you question yourself and feel bad about yourself by making you think that "everyone" else agrees with them about something negative about you. They may make comments such as "everyone else sees it this way" or, "everyone else thinks your behavior is crazy." Over time, this mindfuckery can increase your self-consciousness and self-doubt. What can be worse is when you turn to a once trusted friend or family member to share your side and experience them giving you feedback that is aligned with the narcissist's smear campaign, or you find you lose friends and family because of it.

DARVO

DARVO stands for Deny, Attack, Reverse Victim and Offender (Freyd, 1997). It is a tactic often seen in pathological love relationships when the abuser tries to escape or shift blame for their behavior. It is an aspect of gaslighting and can lead to you questioning everything about your sanity, your worth, and your reality. Here is a breakdown:

- **D**eny: The pathological partner has an uncanny ability to deny anything and everything if it will make them look bad or face consequences, even when presented with cold hard facts to show otherwise. Let's take cheating,

for example. You find a string of text messages on their phone that are clearly flirtatious, sexual in nature, include nude photos, and imply they've been cheating. You confront the person and immediately they deny it. "I'm not cheating on you!" (Despite clear evidence in front of them).
- **A**ttack: Even when caught with evidence, the denial is quickly followed by an attack on you. "How dare you look at my phone! You're so insecure. No wonder your ex divorced you." This may feel confusing and disorienting, as you just caught them doing something wrong, but they are trying to make you feel bad.
- **R**everse **V**ictim & **O**ffender: These last three steps occur after the pathological person has attacked you or your character, and then they try to make you feel like the one who is perpetrating the abuse against them. They may say "you violated my privacy! You have no right to look into my phone. How can I trust you when you are so nosy and always poking around in my life? You are so controlling of me, it's abusive! You should really get some help for that."

My story with Andrew is an example of the DARVO tactic. He denied or ignored the fact that I told him he didn't need to come home early. He then attacked me, telling me I was controlling, and then turned himself into the victim, demanding my apology. This is mindfuckery at its finest, folks.

NARCISSISTIC ABUSE CYCLE

This is an important dynamic to recognize, as it is a telltale sign of narcissistic abuse. This cycle has three phases: idealization, devaluation, and discard. This cycle can occur in short increments of time, which may occur during arguments or conflict. It can also happen over the course of a relationship, eventually leading to cheating, ghosting or abandonment, a breakup, or divorce.

- **Idealization:** The narcissist puts their victim on a pedestal and the love-bombing and mirroring begins. You may feel respected, adored, or loved in this phase. You may feel smitten and loving toward the narcissist, which gives them the supply their ego needs.
- **Devaluation:** At some point, the narcissist realizes you aren't perfect and you're knocked off the pedestal. This may occur when you challenge or disagree with them, give feedback or criticism, or any number of things. It could be something completely benign to most people, but because of the narcissist's fragile ego and hypersensitivity to perceived criticism, you may never even know the trigger for the discard. Narcissists experience dichotomous, black and white thinking, and tend to see people as all good or all bad, with little room for human imperfection. This is where the gaslighting, blame, projection, and mindfuckery begins.
- **Discard:** Finally, you may experience the narcissistic discard. This occurs when you begin to set boundaries, ask for honesty or integrity, or somehow challenge their ridiculous behaviors. You are no longer a supply to the narcissist's ego, and they can drop you in drastic, cold, and unexplained abandonments, or a dramatic situation that forces an end to the relationship. You may be left spinning in heartbreak and confusion, wondering how someone who once proclaimed their love for you could end things in such a quick, cold-hearted manner. To add

salt to your wounds, you may experience the narcissist moving on to a new supply soon after the breakup or discover that they are cheating (new supply).

The mindfuckery in this chapter is only a brief sampling and description of a myriad of methods the narcissistic or toxic person may use to manipulate and harm their victims. They can be incredibly sneaky or subtle or can pierce you like a sword. It is extremely important that you do not dismiss these types of tactics. Many people believe that if they aren't being physically hurt, they are not experiencing an abusive relationship. Nonetheless the reality is, these dynamics constitute emotional, psychological, and verbal abuse, and can leave invisible scars that can last a lifetime if not treated.

PART TWO

INTERNAL RED FLAGS: THE BODY SPEAKS YOUR TRUTH

CHAPTER 5

WHAT MAKES US VULNERABLE?

What comes to mind when you think of a victim of domestic violence? Do you envision a bruised, bloodied, backbone lacking woman who escapes a violent, "wife beater" of a man in the middle of the night? Do you imagine someone who grew up in a dysfunctional home watching her mother get abused, who is simply repeating learned relationship patterns? Maybe you think of someone who bounces from one relationship to the next, who seems to be utterly dependent upon a partner to survive. What about men? Or gay or lesbian couples? Do you think about them as victims of domestic violence? What about a woman who seems to have it all… the "perfect" marriage, the successful career, healthy self-esteem, confidence, and boundaries? Could she fall prey to this?

The truth is, each of these are examples of people who can become victims of domestic violence and pathological love relationships. Most of what we know about intimate partner violence is based on outdated and severely under-researched models of understanding what has been considered "domestic violence," along with decades of stereotypical portrayals of this in Hollywood movies. There is an assumption that only someone who lacks boundaries, confidence, or self-esteem, such as a codependent person, could possibly allow someone to creep their way into their lives and abuse them.

You're about to learn the truth behind what makes people vulnerable to this abuse in this section of the book where we will begin to identify "internal red flags." Your internal red flags are based on two factors. First, we'll look at what makes you more vulnerable to becoming involved in a pathological relationship. This will serve as a red flag you will always keep in mind, whether you are single or in a relationship, as it sets the stage for your risk and vulnerability. Second, we'll explore the internal reactions and symptoms that will help you determine whether you are experiencing a pathological love relationship. I hope to break down these stereotypes so you can become clear on the who, how, and why people can become a victim to pathological partners.

ARE WE ALL JUST CODEPENDENT?

After growing up in a home with a mother and stepfather who were addicts, my role as the oldest child was that of caretaker and parent to my younger siblings. I tried to become the anchor and stability for my family's chaos. Some would see my pattern of becoming a parentified child in my family the root of future enabling, codependent behaviors. I learned to put my needs aside in an attempt to make my mom happy or try to get the attention of my narcissistic stepdad, or my emotionally distant father. It came as no surprise that I ended up in adult relationships where I continued the role of caretaker and people pleaser.

As I was committed to my healing and personal growth, I explored my "codependent" patterns with several well-meaning therapists in my early years. I was told to go to Alateen and Al-Anon meetings in my teens and twenties, where I received support and a solid understanding that it was not my fault nor my role to address the addiction issues in my family. While these meetings were helpful in educating me about addiction and codependency, I felt a sense of shame, believing there was something inherently wrong with me. I did A LOT of work on myself to heal trauma and patterns of codependency I had learned from childhood. Yet, something wasn't sinking in, and I couldn't seem to shake the deeper feelings inside that kept me so tuned in to others' emotions and needs. Despite the personal work, my clinical awareness, and experience, I kept finding myself in one pathological love relationship after another. Something was amiss, but I could not find the missing piece.

In the mental health and pop psychology arenas, codependency is seen as the biggest influence behind a person's involvement in narcissistic abuse and pathological love relationships. Codependency is not a diagnosis in the *DSM-5*, however, has been widely studied and made popular in the field of addiction recovery and pop psychology. In fact, this term has become so widely known that many of us freely use it to describe people who seem dependent or enabling of someone.

The term "codependency" originated in the 12-Step Alcoholics Anonymous model to describe friends, partners, and family members who were enabling an addict to continue using their drug of choice (alcohol, drugs, sex, gambling, etc.). Initially, this idea was groundbreaking, as it helped us understand that addiction was not only a problem with the addict, but that the family was often contributing to the addiction by enabling the addict's disease. In her book, *Another Chance: Hope and Health for the Alcoholic Family*, Susan Wegscheider-Cruise shares a person was considered codependent if they were (a) in a love or marital relationship with an alcoholic, (b) had one or more alcoholic parents or grandparents, or (c) were raised within an emotionally repressed family.

Melody Beattie, author of *Codependent No More*, expanded the concept from the 12-Step model into a broader focus to help us understand our enabled, enmeshed relationships. The concept has now evolved to describe someone who is "addicted" to unhealthy relationships, and in particular, to someone who is abusive, pathological, or addicted. Usually, the focus of codependency recovery is to increase self-love and self-esteem while strengthening your boundaries. Essentially, if you heal your codependency issues and the underlying lack of self-worth and boundaries, you will "fix" yourself, thus your relationships will change.

I wholeheartedly agree that we must examine and change codependent behaviors. Codependency is real and can be significantly damaging to relationships. However, what is typically lacking in this model is a focus on identifying and treating the underlying trauma that creates the low self-worth, the diffuse sense of self, and poor boundaries that underly the codependent behaviors. This concept of blaming codependency is only skimming the surface, which means people are generally not getting the deeper, truly transformational healing needed to break the cycle of dysfunctional or abusive relationships. Codependency is a symptom of trauma, not the problem itself. At its core, codependency is actually a compilation of trauma responses (most often fawning, freezing, flight, and feign), and may also be the emotional and behavioral expression of an anxious attachment, which we will learn more about in future chapters.

When people are simply focused on improving their self-esteem and trying to set boundaries with a narcissist, they may get nowhere since the underlying trauma or attachment response is being ignored. You can try to talk your way into behavior change and repeat positive affirmations all day, but if you have trauma or attachment challenges underlying your codependent patterns, your brain is actually choosing your reactions for you in an effort to keep you safe. You are not consciously deciding it is a great idea to let some jerk of a partner slather you in abusive tirades or to use your face as a punching bag. In that moment, your nervous system has reacted in a way that does not give room for analytical decision-making. Your mind and body receive messages that say: *Kiss ass. Don't move a muscle. Do the dishes and smile even if you are fuming beneath it all. Cover your tears with please and thank you. You are in danger and if you don't do this, you may be seriously injured or die.*

I don't know about you, but I would never consciously choose to allow someone to abuse me. I'm a feminist. I'm a therapist. I can set strong boundaries with people. I have healthy self-esteem. I can see a lot of psychological dynamics unfolding before my eyes, yet when my body senses that I am in danger, I will people please all day if it will keep me safe in that moment. Some may call it codependency, I call it survival, which is ultimately a trauma response.

Furthermore, a sole focus on codependency to explain our involvement in pathological relationships also tends to ignore societal, cultural, biological, and other factors that can influence someone's ability to identify or self-protect against abusive relationships. Codependency is simply a lens with which we can understand these dynamics, but it is not a singular explanation. We must remember that codependency is a trauma problem, not a choice, nor an addiction problem. It also has significant cultural and systemic influences that must be examined.

PERSONALITY SUPER TRAITS: A NEW PERSPECTIVE

Fortunately, we now have research that challenges this notion that codependency is the reason for most people's involvement in abusive relationships. A 2014 study with over 600 female participants conducted by Sandra L. Brown, MA and a team at Purdue University, found that 63 percent of the women interviewed did NOT have adverse childhoods (where they experienced abuse, neglect, or traumatic experiences) that typically led to codependent or dependent behaviors. This research raises the question: why do so many therapists think codependency is to blame? This can be attributed to the hypothesis that mental health clinicians often treat the remaining 37 percent of this group, of whom have backgrounds of trauma and resulting codependent traits. Therefore, clinicians see a trend that leads them to believe that most survivors of these relationships are simply codependent (Brown and Young, 2018).

Brown highlights the astonishing lack of research on how and why we can become victims of this abuse. This common belief that victims suffer from codependency, childhood trauma, or personality disorders such as borderline or dependent personality disorder is rampant. Survivors may even be called sex or love addicts. Pop psychology, with its myriad of non-psychologically trained bloggers, coaches, and YouTubers points the finger at codependency as the main explanation. Brown also found that many of the women interviewed did not fit the common misperceived stereotype of a victim of domestic violence who ends up in a battered women's shelter. Many of these women were well resourced in other areas of their lives and had only suffered trauma from the pathological love relationship.

Brown and her colleagues discovered that instead of codependency being the core explanation behind our involvement in PLRs, a majority of women actually had two particular personality "super traits" in common. This groundbreaking evidence illuminated a new perspective about how and why people may fall prey to these relationships. Super traits are personality characteristics with which we are born, meaning they are hard wired into our nervous system and personalities. Of the super traits identified, the two most common traits of agreeableness and conscientiousness in survivors of pathological relationships were connected to higher rates of vulnerability to relationship abuse by toxic partners. Brown provides detailed descriptions of these two super personality traits:

AGREEABLENESS
- **Empathy:** Generally full of compassion, forgiveness, and the ability to put oneself in another's shoes. This person will feel empathy for even the most abusive humans.
- **Straightforward:** This trait shows a knack for being vulnerable and open to sharing about oneself. There may be

a high degree of authenticity, honesty, and directness in communication.
- **Trust:** This person is generally optimistic about human nature and has faith in the ability for people to change and grow. Because of this, trust may be placed on others before they have earned it.
- **Cooperative:** This is all about playing nice with others. There is a value for reciprocity in relationships, and a desire to support others, share, and collaborate vs. compete.
- **Humble:** This person is usually warm, likable, open, and modest in their self-portrayal.
- **Loyalty:** As an Achilles' heel that can keep a person stuck in the unhealthy relationship, this trait is all about being faithful, committed, and holding integrity in one's relationships, and is clearly a positive trait in other situations in life.
- **Tolerance:** There is a high degree of tolerance for the behaviors and values of others, including that of the pathological person in their life.
- **Giving Nature:** Kind, generous, considerate, and altruistic, this person is focused on giving to others not because they are codependent, but because they have big hearts and giving comes natural to them (Brown and Young, 2018).

CONSCIENTIOUSNESS
- **Dependable and Reliable:** You can depend on this person as they have a high degree of integrity in being there for others.
- **Efficient:** Tends to be a natural problem solver who gets things done with competency and resourcefulness and can be somewhat of a perfectionist.

- **Deliberateness:** This trait is about being diligent, careful, thoughtful, and persevering. Brown notes that survivors can experience confusion about how they ended up in these toxic relationships, as they are usually cautious, thoughtful, and careful about decisions. Unfortunately, the toxic person is usually so good at mirroring what the target needs, wants, or values that it is easy to be manipulated.
- **Organized:** This person can bring order to chaos and while they may lose their natural tendency to be organized if suffering from the trauma of an abusive relationship, this is their natural tendency.
- **Self-disciplined:** Not a quitter, this person will go far beyond what many people can tolerate in life, and unfortunately in a dysfunctional relationship.
- **Achievement Oriented:** Often very focused on achieving goals, these types may do well in career and life. The downside of this trait is that this person can become trapped in trying to reach the never-ending task of satisfying the critical narcissist (Brown and Young, 2018).

A complicating factor typically seen in people with these super traits is that they have a low degree of another super trait called "harm avoidance" (Brown and Young, 2018). The personality trait of harm avoidance describes someone who experiences pessimism, excessive worrying, doubt, fear of uncertainty, and are easily fatigued. People with high degrees of conscientiousness and agreeableness are usually optimistic, self-confident and lack extreme fear and anxiety (so they don't worry about the future as much). They also don't get as fatigued by others as they have the qualities of diligence and perseverance. The negative side of having a low amount of this harm avoidance trait coupled with agreeableness and conscientiousness is that you may lack suspiciousness and can be too trusting and optimistic about others. You may not set boundaries with people who are needy, controlling, or pulling you into their drama. You may not allow yourself to consider the dark side of a person, as you may only focus on the good.

As you can see, these traits tend to have an Achilles' heel quality to them. In many ways, agreeableness and conscientiousness have a positive, prosocial aspect to them, leading to success in life and in many relationships. In fact, leaders such as Gandhi, Martin Luther King Jr., and Nelson Mandela share these traits. However, because these traits are largely unchangeable, as they are hardwired into the personality, they create inevitable risk for future involvement in pathological love relationships.

WHY IT'S IMPORTANT TO KNOW THE DIFFERENCE
Herein lies the problem. Codependency and trauma can and must be addressed through the lens of trauma focused treatment for successful healing and recovery. PLR survivors who begin the relationship with a history of childhood trauma will likely become further traumatized by the PLR and develop complex post-traumatic stress disorder, which is a more chronic and severe form of PTSD (and requires longer-term, specialized therapeutic focus.) Doing work on healing the trauma and patterns of codependency, such as improving boundaries, self-esteem, and self-worth, would be appropriate for this group.

However, for PLR survivors (the majority of women, according to the Purdue study) who do not have adverse, traumatic histories, trying to fit them into a treatment model that sees them as such is overkill, inaccurate, and even stigmatizing. You cannot heal a personality trait. It is not injured or broken. You can only gain awareness and manage it. Now, these survivors may need trauma focused treatment to address the trauma connected to the PLR, but they tend to be more resilient because of these personality traits, and therefore may recover more easily than the other group with childhood histories of trauma.

Personally, this hit the nail on the head. I had a particular experience of having both an adverse childhood history which needed (and had experienced) trauma healing. That work helped me clear up what might have been any codependent patterns. What had not been identified by myself or any therapist, were my super traits of conscientiousness and agreeableness. I was strong, fiercely independent, successful, assertive and able to set boundaries, and had healthy self-esteem, yet my relationships were riddled with narcissistic men. My personality traits were the cause, not codependency or trauma.

It comes as no surprise that codependency can mimic characteristics of these particular super traits. For example, the high degree of tolerance and cooperation in these super traits can be misinterpreted as the "people pleasing" behaviors seen in codependency. Another example is a codependent person will focus on making the relationship work out of a fear of abandonment and a need for approval, whereas someone with these super traits will work on the relationship because they are highly empathic, loyal, committed, persistent, and resourceful. These can be subtle differences that look similar on the surface, but when you explore the roots of the behavior, there are significant differences which require different approaches in order to break the patterns that lead to PLRs.

In survivors with super traits, their behavior in the PLR begins to look like codependency since it is a response to the trauma, manipulation, gaslighting, and coercion experienced. Here are some examples:

- Prior to the PLR, a survivor was capable of meeting their own needs, but seems entirely dependent on their partner and has not been meeting their needs since the PLR trauma began, as they may be forced to only focus on the partner's needs.
- A survivor experiences low self-esteem during and after the PLR after experiencing gaslighting, criticism, devaluing, and lies, however has otherwise had healthy self-esteem (and it often returns after healing from the PLR).
- A survivor experiences denial in the PLR, which is a temporary result of trauma and cognitive dissonance, and not a lifelong pattern of denial as a primary coping strategy.
- A survivor seems to have poor boundaries in the PLR, which is a result of being threatened, controlled, and forced to loosen boundaries, yet they've had strong boundaries up until the PLR, or have them in other areas of their life.
- A survivor has lost trust and faith in others because they've lost trust in the PLR due to the lying and abuse, but has traditionally been a trusting, open hearted person (Brown and Young, 2018).

As you can see, it is important to get clear on whether you have personality super traits, a history of trauma, patterns of codependency, or a mix of all three, as this will give you a clear understanding about how you become vulnerable to PLRs, and a better idea of what type of healing and therapeutic support you may need to recover.

EMPATHS AND HIGHLY SENSITIVE PEOPLE

Many survivors of narcissistic abuse and pathological love relationships identify as empaths and highly sensitive people. According to psychiatrist Dr. Judith Orloff, author of *The Empath's Survival Guide*, empaths have finely tuned emotions, and can pick up on the emotions of others, as well as the energy of their environments. They are spiritually attuned, generous and giving by nature, and supportive listeners. Sometimes empaths struggle to differentiate between others' emotions from their own because of their ability to take on others' emotional states.

Dr. Elaine Aron, author of *The Highly Sensitive Person: How to Thrive When the World Overwhelms You*, states that highly sensitive people (HSPs) are similar to empaths as they share the following traits: a need for alone time, sensitivity to their environment, such as smells, sounds, light, or crowds. Both can share a love for nature, may feel a desire to help others, and can have a rich inner life. HSPs are almost always introverts, meaning they generate their energy from being alone, whereas empaths can be introverts or extroverts (generate their energy from being with others). Empaths are usually HSPs, but not all HSPs are empaths. The difference is that empaths have the ability to feel the emotions of others, whereas a HSP doesn't have this ability, but may be overstimulated or influenced by the environment (or the emotions of people) around them.

Why is this concept of empathy important to consider when dealing with pathological relationships? As you are probably understanding by now, people who have higher degrees of empathy are very caring, considerate, and compassionate people. Someone with a high degree of empathy is more likely to feel compassion and forgiveness for the narcissist or pathological person. Narcissists and sociopaths often have histories of trauma, or they present themselves as the victim. The HSP, empath, agreeable or conscientious person may feel sensitive and cautious around the fragile ego of the narcissist or feel compassion for their poor behavior since they can also sense a deeper emotional wound in the pathological person.

We can delude ourselves into feeling more sensitive to what makes them become monsters than to feeling sensitive to what happens to us when they become monsters. We have big, loving hearts. However, having a big, loving heart doesn't mean we should subject ourselves to abuse. We must learn to care from a distance, and more importantly, we MUST learn to place our compassion in the right place. If you are being bullied or abused, then that means *you must learn to have more compassion for the pain you are experiencing* than for the pain you think your abuser has experienced. Empathy is a beautiful trait. The fact is, we need a lot more of it in our world. But having too much empathy for an abusive person can be dangerous, especially if they are intimately involved in our lives. We must learn to love ourselves more than we love our abusers.

WHAT ELSE MAKES US VULNERABLE?

So far, we've identified several factors that can increase our vulnerability to pathological partners, including having one of the personality super traits of agreeableness or conscientiousness, a history of trauma or codependency, or being an empath or highly sensitive person. There are other factors that can increase our risk. Some of the factors may include:

- Having a history of or current experiences of trauma.
- Having an anxious or disorganized attachment.
- Low self-worth.
- Growing up in a family with abusive, narcissistic, or toxic family members.
- Being disconnected from your body and emotions.
- Narcissistic love-bombing and mirroring.
- Cultural or religious beliefs or values such as "relationships are just hard" or "till death do us part."
- Gaslighting- we are manipulated and brainwashed into doubting our reality.

In the next section of this book, we will explore these vulnerabilities in depth, as we continue to identify the internal red flags that will increase your self-awareness and self-protective factors. The good news is that there is a better warning system which is incredibly reliable, accurate, and highly personal once you've developed it. You don't need the *DSM-5*, or Google for this one. It starts with developing a relationship with you.

CHAPTER 6

THE #1 RED FLAG

Trigger Warning This section contains a potentially triggering story of domestic abuse. If you are sensitive to this because of your own trauma, please skip past my personal story to the section below titled "Cognitive Dissonance."

When I met Ryan, I was vulnerable and learning how to date after a divorce. The love-bombing felt like water in the parched sponge of my heart. The relationship started with that magical, soul mate quality love, of course. But the truth is, Ryan was a grandiose narcissist. I knew this because he was my partner for almost three years, and despite seeing so many red flags, I had lost myself in the relationship. The fact I dismissed those red flags that might have prevented so much heartbreak for me is likely a large part of why I'm writing this book. I saw them, however I kept questioning myself and my reality, just as one does when you have personality super traits coupled up with the gaslighting, love-bombing, and trauma of a pathological love relationship. A part of me recognized his narcissism, yet another part of me saw such a wounded person beneath his behavior, for whom I felt so much empathy and compassion. He had suffered significant childhood neglect, abuse, and lost his parents at an early age. I wanted to believe he was simply behaving "badly" because of his trauma.

Over time, his mask wore off and I began to see the real Ryan. He got fired from every job, but it was always someone else's fault. He would explode in anger over the smallest things. Sometimes he would disappear for twenty-four hours for no reason, sending me into a spiral of anxiety and panic, to the point that I even called all of the emergency rooms in town searching for him. He'd create a dramatic fight or threaten suicide whenever I had an important event. He manipulated me into loaning him money, never paying it back. He even manipulated me into buying him a car, promising he had the money to pay me back a week later, yet I never received a dime.

Word salad was his favorite form of communication, as it seemed like he picked arguments just for the thrill of the fight. After endless hours of mindfuckery, I would eventually become distraught and emotionally dysregulated. The moment I sunk to my lowest, he switched from evil Mr. Hyde into caring Dr. Jekyll, comforting me in his arms while I sobbed. He nurtured and caressed me, love-bombing me back into forgiveness and connection. I was disgusted with him, yet more so with myself for falling right back into his grip. He tore me down intentionally just to swoop back in and become my rescuer. It was an intoxicating, dark, and toxic pattern that kept me hooked, yet completely traumatized.

After two years of this insanity, I was stuck in a spiral of indecision about whether to leave him. We'd break up, reconcile, repeat. The cycle was magnetic. In one of our reconciliation moments, we decided to take a trip to Mexico, and in my mind, it was a last-ditch effort to decide whether I would stay in this relationship. On our last day there, we took an infamous "booze cruise," where Ryan proceeded to drink himself into a stupor in the hot sun. We returned to our hotel room late in the day, and I went to the bathroom to shower. When I came out, I found him passed out. At first, I was startled, worried, and tried to wake him. He mumbled a few words and fell back to sleep. I was starving so I left him a note that I was going to the hotel restaurant to get dinner and would return.

A half hour later, as I rode up the elevator with food in hand, the doors opened to Ryan standing in the hallway. Wearing only his shorts, his red, sweaty, bare-chested body was tight with rage. His eyes looked completely black and there was white saliva bubbling at the corners of his mouth. He lunged at me before I could even leave the elevator, pulling me into the hotel room, slamming the heavy door behind him. My mind had no time to think, but my body was instantly trembling as I handed him the plate of food. "I just went to get you some food. I thought you would feel better if you ate."

He snarled "why would you leave me? I can never trust you! Who were you with?"

I calmly stated "Ryan, I was only gone for a half an hour. You wouldn't wake up and I was hungry. I brought you food."

He snarled "you're a fucking liar. I know you were fucking someone. You fucking bitch. How could you be so fucking selfish? You took advantage of me falling asleep and went and cheated on me!"

This began what became hours of him standing over me, yelling, threatening, and belittling me. At first, I tried to reason with him, soothe him, yet I soon realized this just escalated his rage. I finally curled up in a fetal position in the corner of the hotel room, my mind searching for ideas on how to escape from the tenth floor of a high-rise hotel room. I could jump, or I could run for the only door, which he was guarding. I held my head in my hands and whimpered quiet cries, avoiding any attempts to argue or fight back. I began thinking of how my children would live their lives without their mother, as I feared for my life.

At some point, he left me and began urinating in the bathroom. Something stealth and courageous grew within me as I tip-toed to the exit, praying he didn't notice as I walked past the open bathroom door. I took a deep breath and darted across to the door, but his adrenaline-fueled swiftness matched my own. He ran from the toilet with his shorts around his ankles, dripping piss across his legs and the floor as he ran toward me. He picked me up by my arms and lunged me back into the bathroom, throwing me into the shower like a rag doll, limp, and completely powerless. I lay there on the cold wet floor, feeling simultaneously numb yet seething in pain.

"You crazy fucking bitch! You're so selfish! You were going to leave and get me in trouble? WHAT THE FUCK! You would put me in jail in Mexico? You'd send me to jail to get raped? You know I was sexually abused when I was a kid." I laid there, silently weeping, my body frozen on the hard cold floor.

Suddenly I heard a knock on the door. Ryan quickly threw on a t-shirt and opened it. I heard his voice, however it seemed as if someone else had stepped into his body; he was laughing and calmly talking to the hotel staff who asked if everything was ok. Ryan graciously apologized "Oh, we are so sorry! My girlfriend had too many cervezas and was having too much fun, if you know what I mean." The man at the door laughed along with him, as if they were part of the unspoken brotherhood, the good ol' boys club. I imagined them giving each other a grin and that knowing wink as my rescuer dismissed the suspicions of chaos behind our closed doors.

There I was, being given an opportunity to escape, to liberate myself from this terrorist, and I said nothing. I froze. For a moment, I did consider what would happen to him if he was arrested. My mind flipped through the possibilities of him being stuck in a prison for years in a foreign country (likely based on one too many stereotypical movie scenes). I huddled in the corner in silence as this moment became forever imprinted in my psyche. My shame deepened as I questioned my strange reaction. *Why did I stay silent? Why didn't I run for the door? Why in the hell did I care about what happened to him? I was fearing for my life!* I was completely baffled and disgusted by my reaction.

At some point we both fell asleep. The next day, I examined the bruises on my arms and back in the mirror. I was shocked. I had never been physically hurt by a man before. I was too numb to feel any emotion. He looked at me and said, "you better not do anything stupid today to get me thrown into prison." I said nothing, my body joined him in complicit silence as we began our journey home through a cab ride, airport security, two flights, and past hundreds of people who could have helped. But somehow, I felt frozen and unable to even muster a whisper of an SOS to the world around me. I didn't want him to go to prison and imagined the horror for him, as I completely ignored the trauma I had just endured.

COGNITIVE DISSONANCE

There is one particular glaring red flag that far surpasses any of the red flags we'll explore in this book is highly indicative of your involvement in a PLR. *Cognitive dissonance* (CD) is the "hallmark symptom" of a pathological love relationship (Brown, 2009). Cognitive dissonance is defined as a psychological conflict resulting from incongruous beliefs and attitudes that are held simultaneously (Merriam-Webster Dictionary Online Ed., 2022). This process creates an internal state of anxiety, and a need to resolve the conflicting beliefs by essentially choosing one to align with as their truth.

Most survivors experience this in the form of confusing thoughts such as, "I love him/I fear him," or "I can't stand to be away from her/I can't stand to be with her." They will constantly compare and contrast the memories and experience with their partner, struggling to arrive at a decision about what to do about the relationship. Over time, this dynamic strengthens and can destroy a survivor's sense of self-worth as they begin to feel confusion and shame around their decision to remain with a pathological partner despite the abusive behavior they endure. Survivors with the super traits of agreeableness and conscientiousness are most vulnerable to and affected by CD (Brown and Young, 2009).

I struggled with whether to share this story about Ryan with you, as it is deeply personal, and I experienced shame about it for many years. However, my intention is to show you the destructive power of cognitive dissonance. Most of all, I share this to help you free yourself from any shame you may hold for your involvement in a relationship such as this. My cognitive dissonance began within months of the relationship, as I began to see the inconsistencies in his behavior. The more red flags I witnessed, the stronger the dissonance became until I found myself lost and unable to think clearly about leaving him. I saw the red flags, yet I stayed, feeling shame for betraying my own relationship standards. I felt horrible about myself, thanks to the dissonance paired with the gaslighting I endured. I truly believed no one would love me if I left. *He was the only one.* As a therapist, I was disgusted with myself. It took a lot of deep trauma work to repair my wounds after I finally left him. You are about to learn exactly why you get entangled in a PLR, and how it can be so destructive.

Cognitive dissonance occurs when we begin to witness inconsistency and unpredictability in a partner, as they no longer seem like the person we believed them to be, or their actions no longer match their words. In *Women Who Love Psychopaths: Inside the Relationships of Inevitable Harm with Psychopaths, Sociopaths & Narcissists* (2018), Brown and Young describe the progression of cognitive dissonance in a survivor as:

- Inconsistency in a survivor's thought's (he's loving/he's cruel. She's honest/she's lying)
- Inconsistency in a survivor's feelings (I adore him/I fear him. I trust her/I don't trust her)
- Inconsistency in a survivor's behavior (I am being abused, but I stay. I won't tolerate cheating, but my partner is cheating and I stay)

As a survivor begins to experience the first signs of pathology and inconsistency in their partner, they may try to change the way they think about the disturbing behavior. This is especially true if a survivor has the agreeableness super trait. The survivor's thinking may lean toward hope and optimism (part of the agreeableness trait), as they focus on the positive aspects in the partner, while dismissing the new and concerning side of their partner. Survivors may have a tendency to assume other people are like them, with strong morals, compassion, and empathy. Cognitive dissonance is like having tunnel vision, where the survivor will focus on information about the partner that aligns with their beliefs, outright dismissing information that conflicts with their beliefs. For example, when catching your partner in a lie, instead of becoming concerned about his lying, you think "it wasn't that big of a lie. He's so much better than the other men I've dated" (Brown and Young, 2018).

As the relationship progresses, cognitive dissonance produces conflicting feelings in a survivor. The intense love-bombing and mirroring that occurs can create euphoric feelings of love and safety. Yet as the pathology rears its ugly head, the survivor begins to feel fear, anxiety, distrust, betrayal, and other painful emotions in response to the pathological partner's behavior. This behavioral inconsistency strengthens the cognitive dissonance, and the survivor is caught in a confusing web of mixed emotions and thoughts about the relationship.

Finally, the longer a survivor has endured the Jekyll and Hyde inconsistencies of their partner, the deeper the dissonance becomes as it merges with their basic identity and sense of self. This is where the survivor may begin to do things that are against their own moral code, such as enduring physical abuse by their partner, despite having a lifelong belief that relationships should never be violent. This is also when the trait of conscientiousness aggravates the dissonance, as this trait has elements that make a survivor feel dedicated and loyal to the relationship at all costs. Brown shares the worst part of dissonance for a survivor is for them to face who they have become in the PLR, as they are no longer aligned with their morals and beliefs. They tend to feel like they had lost control of themselves in the relationship and compared it to feeling like an addiction (Brown and Young, 2018).

Studies done by The Institute for Relational Harm Reduction & Public Pathology Education have shown survivors with high degrees of conscientiousness will suffer the most from cognitive dissonance. The reason for this is because this trait is all about having integrity and strong values and morals and living in alignment with them. When a survivor comes to terms with the fact they are living with the darkness of a PLR, it creates a "self-perceptual injury" where they no longer feel like themselves, nor are they able to connect to their once established internal resources that would have helped them navigate through and out of an abusive relationship such as this. The agreeableness trait adds fuel to this fire, as a survivor wants to give many "second chances" and will continue to tolerate the abusive behavior (Brown, 2017).

The Institute also states the effects of PLR cognitive dissonance can reduce the brain's executive functioning skills, which include decision-making, reasoning, judgment, memory, planning, organizing, and complex tasks. These skills are needed to evaluate the confusing behavior of the pathological partner, or to create a strategy to leave the relationship. They are required to get clarity on the relationship through analyzing, reasoning, and making decisions based on the experiences of abuse. CD becomes more than just an internal conflict. It can affect the neurology of the brain in the same ways trauma and PTSD affect the brain (Brown and Young, 2018). It isn't uncommon for survivors to experience significant challenges or setbacks in their careers and daily functioning because of these trauma-induced brain injuries.

THE TRAUMA BOND

In his 2019 book, *The Betrayal Bond: Breaking Free of Exploitative Relationships,* Patrick Carnes, PhD, defined a trauma bond as "the misuse of fear, excitement, sexual feelings, and the sexual physiology to entangle another person." The intense love-bombing, devaluation, and discard the survivor experiences with a pathological partner creates a system of intermittent reinforcement, which is *THE* most powerful behavioral motivator. To understand it's power, all you have to do is look to the gambling industry, which is based on the concept of intermittent reinforcement. Slot machines and card games keep people hooked in a cycle of dropping money into a slot as they wait for the occasional win. Most people suffer more losses but continue to engage in the addictive cycle. This pattern is similar to the inconsistent and unpredictable moments of love-bombing that occur in the abuse of the PLR.

The vacillation between love and abuse the survivor experiences also creates cognitive dissonance, which builds and reinforces the trauma bond, becoming a powerful magnet that draws one into the arms of pathology. This explains why it takes women an average of seven attempts to successfully leave an abusive relationship. *Seven attempts.* If you have had the experience of the cycle of breaking up and reconciling your relationship multiple times, and experiencing cognitive dissonance about your partner, the relationship, or yourself, this is your red flag, and it is very, very red.

SIGNS OF A TRAUMA BOND

How do you know if you or someone you know is experiencing a trauma bond? Some telltale signs include:

- Experiencing cognitive dissonance about a partner's "good" and "bad" behavior (and likely overlooking the "bad" behavior)
- Justifying or defending the abuse to yourself or others
- Lying or covering up for abuse
- Distancing from friends, family, or therapists who attempt to help or ask about abuse
- Becoming hostile or defensive if someone tries to stop the abuse (hostile toward the person stopping it, not the abuser)
- Agreeing with the abuser that you should be abused or deserved it
- Returning to the abuser several times despite being hurt
- Holding on to hope for the future with the abusive person, hoping they'll change or apologize (despite no signs that they've actually improved, or maintained any changes over time)

In my case, I knew I was in a trauma bond with Ryan by that point in the relationship. Even with all of my awareness as a therapist, the intense cognitive dissonance that had developed over a couple of years with him, overpowered my rational mind, keeping me stuck, confused, and unsure of whether to leave or give him another chance. The trauma bond gave me pause in that moment in the hotel room when I could have escaped into safety, but for a moment, I had more sympathy for him and his potentially traumatic experience in jail than I had for me and my own safety. Part of me knew what I *should* have done, however I was experiencing significant trauma that impacted my ability to choose *me* in that moment. Crazy as it may sound, my focus was on his safety and well-being, and the desire to spare him from a jail sentence.

The cognitive dissonance I experienced over time went something like this: I loved and cared for this man for almost three years, yet I feared him. I am a therapist who has deep compassion for people with trauma and I would never want someone to experience more trauma…so I couldn't become the person who created more trauma for him by sending him to jail. People who get fired from every job and blame others clearly have some issues going on, but I continued to support him financially, thinking he'd get his act together someday (and I felt shame for enabling this behavior in him). I help empower women to leave abusive relationships in my work, however I couldn't empower myself to leave my own relationship. I felt incredible shame with my decision to stay with this man, despite the horrible behaviors I experienced. Every attempt to leave him was met with a feeling of panic and despair, and the cognitive dissonance would reel me back in with thoughts like *you've never felt love like this before. He's your soul mate. No one else will love you like he does.*

Sandra L. Brown, MA and her team at the Institute for Relational Harm Reduction have done extensive work to help us understand the trauma bond. In their Cognitive Dissonance & Trauma Bonds Study (2017), these dynamics of the trauma bond were identified:

- The intermittent reinforcement of the abuse and love-bombing creates changes in the chemistry of the brain, which, as we've learned about living under the influence of trauma, can create deep, lasting change in your thoughts, feelings, and behaviors.
- The survivor interacts with the Jekyll and Hyde personality of the narcissist or pathological partner, where experiencing the love-bombing and abuse creates a confusing state of cognitive dissonance. This creates a state of confusion and paralysis in the survivor, as the cognitive dissonance makes it difficult to see the "whole" of the pathological partner.
- This state of cognitive dissonance can also lead to a freeze trauma response, where the survivor becomes immobile, struggling to make decisions about the relationship because they are confused about who the partner really is- good or bad, loving or abusive.
- Experiencing cognitive dissonance and becoming irrationally bonded to a person who abuses you is a trauma in and of itself.
- A trauma bond cannot simply be broken because it just explains a type of relationship that exists, and the resulting dynamics of reinforcement that created the relationship.
- In order to help someone break a trauma bond, they must work to identify and heal the cognitive dissonance that has been created around the relationship.

STUCK IN A TRAUMA BOND? TRY THIS.

If you are experiencing a trauma bond, therapy is highly recommended. It can be very beneficial in helping you resolve the cognitive dissonance and trauma that may be keeping you paralyzed in indecision about your relationship. We'll continue exploring more healing and recovery practices later, but here are a few practices that can also help:

- **See the reality, not the fantasy.** Try to become an objective witness to your partner's behavior, I suggest keeping a journal and listing your experiences. You may find that simply listing, vs. freely writing, processing, and expressing yourself in a journal is easier. The process of journaling may can be triggering, so pay attention to how this experience feels to you and do this only if it helps you. If this works for you, it can be powerful to review the list over time to help you see the "forest through the trees," or the cycle of abuse you are experiencing. It can help decrease cognitive dissonance as well.
- **Stay present focused.** Holding on to dreamy promises once stated by the narcissist in the presence of abuse is cognitive dissonance at its finest. Dreamy promises of the ideal future together, or that your partner will change are the ingredients for a love-bombing cake.
- **Go no contact.** If at all possible, end ALL contact with the narcissist or pathological partner. This includes a rule of no social media "stalking" or following them or their friends and family. Every contact you have re-engages your brain into the cycle with them and will simply prolong your healing. *Note: simply going no contact with no further work on healing the trauma created by the relationship is not an effective way to break a trauma

bond. Breaking contact is ONLY ONE STEP in the healing process.
- **If it walks like a duck and talks like a duck, it probably is a duck.** This little metaphor is good to keep in your head. If you see or experience disturbing, abusive, suspicious, and crazymaking things, you are not making this up. Trust what you see, hear, and experience. Again, see the whole of this person, pay attention to the reality, not just what you want to see.
- **Use the law of balance.** Remember a symptom of trauma during or after an abusive, narcissistic relationship can be holding on to or fantasizing about all of the positive aspects of the relationship, because your brain has experienced those things. But your brain has also experienced trauma and negative experiences. You must balance them out. When you begin fantasizing about the good, write down a list and for every good thing you remember, balance it out with a negative experience. This is especially true for those of you with agreeableness and conscientious super traits who are optimistic and trusting.
- **Practice positive self-talk:** Abuse can lower a person's self-esteem and make them feel they cannot be without the abusive person. Noticing negative self-talk and challenging with positive alternatives can start to change this. A helpful technique can be to ask yourself "who's voice is this?" when negative self-talk begins to spiral. If you think about it, no one is born with that voice in their head. It is likely the voice of a critical parent, your abusive partner, society, social media, etc. Once you identify whose negative voice it is, begin to work on finding your own.
- **Stay open.** As we've learned, a trauma bond can lead to isolation and dismissal of feedback from friends and

family. Try to stay open to feedback, listen to the concerns of others, and take it to heart, especially if the feedback is coming from people who have always been supportive and loving toward you. They may be seeing things you can no longer see because of the trauma you've endured.
- **Seek trauma therapy with a PLR trained therapist, ideally with someone who practices EMDR.** I cannot emphasize this enough.

People who have never experienced an abusive relationship are often perplexed at how someone could defend some of the dreadful behaviors of a perpetrator. This dynamic is deeply misunderstood. Most coaches, bloggers, and even therapists lack the specific knowledge of how and why a trauma bond develops. Often, the advice is to go no contact with the abuser, however, this doesn't actually "break" the trauma bond. It just creates physical space between two people, yet doesn't offer healing for the internal, psychological, emotional, traumatic dynamics that underly the trauma bond. The trauma bond is a dynamic within the survivor that must be acknowledged and healed. Experiencing a trauma bond is a clear red flag that you are in an abusive, toxic, or dysfunctional relationship. The state of paralysis and indecision formed by cognitive dissonance is incredibly destructive, and if ignored, could lead to years, if not decades of abuse. If you are experiencing this dynamic, it is crucial to seek support so you can heal.

CHAPTER 7

THE BODY SPEAKS YOUR TRUTH: THE LANGUAGE OF TRAUMA

Claudia and Ben were high school sweethearts and had been married for twenty-two years. She was a stay-at-home mom until their three children graduated from high school and went on to college. As PTA president and classroom volunteer, she was known by her friends as the mother who would always step in to help. After her kids left for college, she began working as a para-professional in a local school. Ben owned a construction company and had been the sole provider for their family for two decades. He was a strict disciplinarian, and his children obeyed his rules out of fear of his anger. They turned to Claudia for nurturing, but she had learned to show this only when Ben was gone, as he didn't like her "spoiling them." This caused Claudia significant feelings of guilt, yet she complied to avoid more conflict with him.

Ben controlled their money, only giving Claudia an allowance for groceries, gas, and basic necessities. He told her she could have her own money when she got a job, yet even when she began earning an income, he continued to limit her access to their money. Claudia accepted this and said she "wasn't good with money anyway." Ben frequently criticized her, called her lazy, complaining that she didn't earn enough money.

After a long day at work, Claudia would come home to clean the house and make Ben's favorite meal for dinner. As the time approached for him to arrive each night, she would feel herself rushing frantically around the house to make everything perfect, feeling her heart racing and a jittery, panicky feeling. She'd greet him with hugs and a glass of his favorite scotch within minutes of him walking in the door. Ben usually bragged about his daily successes which usually involved bullying one of his employees. He rarely asked her about her day, however, would comment on the clutter he saw on the countertop in the kitchen, or the meal was too salty or not hearty enough. After dinner, he'd retreat to the living room to spend the evening drinking his scotch and watching tv while Claudia cleaned the dishes and deep cleaned some part of the kitchen. Claudia rarely asked for support from anyone, working diligently at school and home. Staying busy, being indispensable to everyone, and keeping her home in order were of primary concern for her.

When her youngest child left home, Claudia said she felt depressed and lost, realizing she had no purpose since her children were gone. She shared a mix of emotions and experiences about her marriage. She resented his need for control and constant criticism. She suspected he had cheated on her with a coworker, however every time she grew suspicious, he would go into a rage, somehow leaving her feeling guilty and ashamed of her suspicions. He had even punched her several times throughout the years. Claudia said she wished she could have spending money to buy some new clothes for work but said "he knows I'm really bad with money, so I understand why he takes charge of our finances. I don't trust myself to not spend it all at Target!"

Sometimes she'd proclaim "I'm so lucky. Honestly, he's been so good to me. He worked hard so I could be a stay-at-home mom all these years. I had it so good compared to my friends who had to work. And I can't imagine not having him in my life. He just has this presence that makes me feel so safe with him."

Other times, she'd break down in tears about him spending two hours yelling at her, saying "I need to leave him. I can't be treated this way anymore. This isn't the person I married."

Claudia described feeling constantly anxious and jumpy. She would startle easily if she heard an angry tone in anyone's voice and would sometimes become so anxious before he arrived home from work that she'd feel like she was "losing her mind" because her heart would race, she'd become sweaty and pace the house in fear. She struggled to focus at work, unable to turn off the thoughts and memories of Ben's explosions. Claudia's body knew what her mind was not willing or was unable to process yet.

POST-TRAUMATIC STRESS DISORDER

Depending on how soon your partner's "mask slips off," you may experience an early trauma reaction based on something horrible your partner does, or it could take several months to years to develop. If you had post-traumatic stress disorder (PTSD), or complex PTSD prior to the relationship you may not realize your symptoms are exacerbated in the PLR. Yet, many people who encounter a PLR may have no history of significant trauma experiences (although the truth is, we've all experienced some degree of trauma in our lives), and their involvement with a person who lacks empathy, and a conscience becomes their first exposure to significant trauma.

The example of Claudia shows many classic signs of trauma, as well as the cognitive dissonance commonly seen in survivors of PLRs. People who have never been involved with a narcissist or pathological partner are often surprised and confused when hearing someone like Claudia who seems to perseverate with indecision about someone whom the rest of us can clearly see is harming them. However, what outsiders may see as clear (this person's partner is a total jerk and they should leave) can be incredibly confusing and disorienting to the victim of a PLR.

According to Sandra L. Brown, MA, 90 percent of PLR survivors have some degree of trauma symptoms, and approximately 50–75 percent of them have diagnosable post-traumatic stress disorder (PTSD) or complex PTSD commonly described as the "aftermath." It is worth noting here that the newfound popularity of narcissistic abuse coaching is filled with coaches and survivors who have no clinical experience in working with trauma. Even among trained mental health professionals, trauma is still not widely recognized nor treated appropriately. Furthermore, PLR survivors tend to have a unique, atypical presentation of PTSD symptoms that trained mental health professionals may overlook if they aren't properly trained in working with PLR survivors. Why is this important? Because survivors can be experiencing debilitating trauma symptoms and attempting to seek therapeutic help but may end up finding little relief from their symptoms which can lead to a return to a PLR.

It is important to know trauma exists on a continuum, and it is also highly subjective. No two people will experience trauma in the same way. There are also different types of trauma disorders, depending on the length of time the person is experiencing symptoms. It is normal to experience many of these symptoms for several days, and even up to a month after a traumatic experience, which is called an acute trauma reaction. For symptoms that persist for longer than a month, the diagnosis of PTSD is given. Chronic, long-term trauma, such as childhood abuse, war, or long-term relationship trauma can turn into complex PTSD.

GENERAL SYMPTOMS OF PTSD INCLUDE:
- Feeling panicked or fearful when being reminded of the abuse, or sometimes for no reason at all
- Difficulty sleeping
- Difficulty concentrating
- Memory issues, not remembering traumatic events
- Nightmares
- Flashbacks (realistic memories of traumatic events that may feel real in the moment)

- Intrusive thoughts (that come to mind at any time, and you have a hard time stopping them)
- Hypervigilance, always on guard
- Startling easily
- Anger, and irritability
- Avoidance of people, places, or things that remind you of the abuse
- Feeling emotionally numb
- Difficulty controlling emotions
- Imagining the worst case scenarios and feeling hopeless about the future
- Zoning out or dissociative
- Suicidal thoughts / fantasies
- Loss of interest in things that you enjoy
- Feelings of guilt, blame, and shame
- The *DSM-5* indicates that in order to be diagnosed with PTSD, a person must be:
- exposed to death,
- threatened death,
- actual or serious injury,
- or actual or threatened sexual violence by directly experiencing the trauma, witnessing it, indirectly by learning a close relative or friend was exposed to trauma, or they suffered repeated or extreme indirect exposure to the trauma (American Psychological Association, 2013).

The problem is many PLR survivors never experience this degree of threat in their relationships, yet they are experiencing many of the other symptoms of PTSD. This may cause some therapists to miss the underlying trauma present in a survivor, which also leads to misdiagnosis. Furthermore, some survivors are labeled with borderline or dependent personality disorder, bipolar disorder, or codependency, again missing the underlying trauma (Brown and Young, 2018). We must view cognitive dissonance along with other symptoms of PTSD as indeed, trauma, and treat it accordingly. If you are in therapy or coaching with someone who does not understand this, it is in your best interest to seek help with a trained trauma professional who understands PLRs.

Traditionally, a therapist will look for memories, intrusive thoughts, and flashbacks of *negative* events in order to diagnose and treat PTSD. However, in PLRs, because of love-bombing and CD, survivors also experience *positive* memories associated with the relationship. What is crucial to understand here is the positive memories are actually considered traumatic by the PLR survivor and are part of the cognitive dissonance. Furthermore, PLR survivors may easily recall positive memories, whereas a therapist may look for the typical PTSD symptoms of difficulty remembering the negative memories. Therapists may only focus on addressing the negative memories, but the positive memories need as much attention and trauma processing, as they can lead to ongoing distress, CD, and a return to the PLR. Brown and Young identify this unique presentation of PTSD here:

ATYPICAL SYMPTOMS OF PTSD IN PLR SURVIVORS:
- Ruminating thoughts about positive memories or feelings along with the negative memories
- Replaying the trauma in the form of thinking about love-bombing or positive experiences in the relationship, vs. only replaying negative memories

- Flashbacks of positive memories which invoke longing and emotional pain, vs. flashbacks of only negative memories
- "Dreams" of positive memories, but are actually to be considered as intrusive nightmares
- Telling stories about the abuse to seek validation as a sign of replaying the trauma and cognitive dissonance
- Avoidance of reminders of both positive and negative events to help avoid cognitive dissonance
- Instead of having difficulty remembering events, may hold strong memories of positive events
- Troubling thoughts about the event can be both negative and positive
- Loss of interest in activities caused by trying to avoid cognitive dissonance, vs. being simply being depressed
- Distorted feelings come from cognitive dissonance vs. distorted feelings of shame and guilt
- Negative thoughts about oneself and the world caused by cognitive dissonance
- Thoughts of both good and bad events vs. only thinking about negative events

As you can see, the focus on the positive memories of the relationship could be deceiving for a therapist or coach who are unaware of this unique presentation of trauma. This is why working with professionals who are trained in PLR dynamics is so important.

THE FOUR FS OF TRAUMA
In an ideal world, our bodies would remain in a fairly relaxed or a calm state most of the time. In moments of stress or fear, our nervous system has a miraculous

mechanism called a *trauma response* which is designed to protect us from danger and ultimately survive. In this ideal world, after the threat is eliminated, we would return to our baseline of calm. Unfortunately, when we are confronted with threats, or even the highly stressful world \we live in, our bodies are often experiencing more of these trauma responses than are healthy.

These trauma responses consist of four different types: fight, flight, freeze, or fawn. Many of you have likely heard of *fight* or *flight*, but most people are not aware that we actually have two other responses, *freeze* and *fawn*. Pete Walker, MA, author of 2013's *Complex PTSD: From Surviving to Thriving: A Guide and Map for Recovering from Childhood Trauma* has described freeze and fawn as other survival strategies for those experiencing complex PTSD, a condition developed from long-term, repeated trauma such as ongoing childhood abuse or domestic violence (such as in a PLR), or living in a war zone. People who experience chronic trauma can develop one or more of these responses as a primary coping style, where it tends to permeate their way of responding to life in general, and especially to stressors or trauma.

Living with chronic trauma is exhausting at the least, and can be devastating to the mental, physical, emotional, and spiritual well-being of a person. People who endure PLRs for long periods of time will likely be experiencing one or more of these responses. It is important to understand these survival strategies so we can identify we are experiencing trauma, and ultimately help ourselves find safety and healing. Here we'll explore each trauma response:

FIGHT

Andrew has many enemies. When he becomes angry, he yells, slams doors, and sometimes becomes physically violent. He grew up in a home where he was physically abused by his father, and by the time he was a teenager, they engaged in fist fights over the slightest disagreements. Andrew was a bully at school, often getting suspended for fighting with his peers. Now that Andrew is an adult, he still reacts with aggression, even with work colleagues and his wife. They walk on eggshells around him, fearing his anger.

Andrew's behavior is an example of the fight response. The goal of fight is to protect yourself and survive *through conflict*. The body will experience a rush of adrenaline, and a person may engage in fighting, yelling, intimidating, or controlling others. People may have an explosive temper or anger, aggressive expressions of emotion, along with increased heart rate, muscle tension, rapid or shallow breathing, trembling, and sweating. It can also manifest as racing thoughts and worry.

FLIGHT

Mikayla is always on the go. She has an endless list of projects, is always stressed and rushing from one thing to the next. She can spend hours perfecting projects at work, doing more than necessary in order to get the job done right. Her house is meticulous, as she often comes home after a long day at work and begins cleaning. She feels exhausted but unable to rest. She's married to a narcissist who keeps her on edge with his criticism and control.

Mikayla's behavior is an example of the flight response, which serves to protect us and help us survive *through escape*. Some people may physically leave or hide from a threatening situation. Flight can also make it hard for people to rest, as they may seem constantly busy, rushing, or seem on edge and panicked. Often these people can be workaholics or perfectionists. Flight can have many of the same symptoms of fight, such as increased heart rate, muscle tension, trembling, sweating, and obsessive, worried thinking.

FREEZE

Daniel experienced severe abuse and neglect as a child. He describes the feeling of leaving his body when his father was beating him and watching the abuse from above. He can sit in his room alone for hours doing nothing and has a difficult time concentrating on tasks as he "zones out," especially when feeling stressed or reminded of his abuse. He struggles to make decisions and lacks confidence in himself to reach goals.

Daniel is experiencing the freeze response, which has the goal of protection and survival *through "dissociation."* We all dissociate at times, as even daydreaming is a mild form of dissociation. However, people who've experienced trauma can experience more intense forms of this coping mechanism and may feel like they are detaching from their body or environment, or feel like things aren't real. People sometimes describe an experience of feeling like they leave their body and watch a trauma occurring from a distance. Being in a freeze response may lead to an inability to make decisions, feeling constant stress, being passive or feeling fear of making even small steps forward in life. Physical symptoms may include a slow heart rate and breathing, blank facial expression, low blood pressure, and the "deer in the headlights" look with constricted pupils in the eyes.

FAWN

Amelia grew up with a narcissistic mother and learned to be in perfect compliance with her mother's unrealistic expectations. She could sense the mood her mother was in the minute she came home from work each day and would find ways to help her relax if she was stressed. She became a cheerleader, learned French, and even wore clothes her mother liked even though she hated all of these things. Disagreeing with her mother would lead to criticism, anger, and conflict. As an adult, she tries to make everyone happy, struggling with setting boundaries.

Amelia is experiencing the fawning response, which has the goal of protection and survival *through extreme people pleasing or placating others*. This response is the foundation for codependent behaviors. It can also be confused with super traits of agreeableness and conscientiousness. Fawners tend to be good at anticipating others' needs, are over complementary or nice to avoid conflict, and struggle with boundaries and saying "no." They often struggle to express their thoughts and feelings and may worry about how others perceive them. This response involves feeling numb, cut off from your own needs, and a general disconnection from body sensations. In an extreme case, it may lead to derealization and depersonalization symptoms where a person may feel like their body isn't part of them, or the world around them isn't real (Schwartz, 2021).

LOVING UNDER THE INFLUENCE OF TRAUMA

People in abusive relationships may experience any and all of these responses at any given time, depending on the circumstances of each moment and the overall tone of the relationship. What's most important to remember about these responses is that they are not conscious. They are instinctual survival responses coming from our nervous system, with the sole purpose of keeping us safe and alive. They are not meant to be slow, analytical, thoughtful decisions. In fact, the prefrontal cortex, the part of our brain that is responsible for analytical, rational thought goes off-line in a moment of threat, and our amygdala, which is responsible for survival, takes over, making the best decision for our survival in the moment.

Many trauma survivors I have worked with over the years, experience guilt and shame over moments when the amygdala chose the best survival strategy for them in the moment of crisis, but in retrospect they wished they would have done something different. An example is a rape survivor who experienced a freeze response during the rape. Her amygdala decided that fighting back or running would be too dangerous in that moment, so the body shut down into a dissociative freeze response until the rape was over and she could escape. Later, the survivor may feel guilt for not fighting or fleeing, thinking she "allowed" it to happen. This is not true. The nervous system made the decision for her. It was not conscious. It was survival.

It might help to consider these survival responses in the context of how they helped us as cave people. If you are walking through the woods one day and see a bear approaching, what do you think happens? If we stopped and took time to think about the best strategy to survive, we could end up wounded or dead. Instead, the nervous system makes an immediate decision for us. It tells us to run and climb the nearest tree, to freeze, or to throw your arms in the air and yell at the bear. We don't have time to stop and think about the size of the bear, whether there is a cave around the bend, or if we have a weapon in our backpack. We only get to analyze what occurred after the threat is over and our bodies have returned to a state of equilibrium and safety. This response is a miraculous mechanism that is designed to keep us alive. We get to use the analytical, rational part of our brain to think things through when we are not feeling threatened.

When you are faced with chronic abuse by a partner or family member, your nervous system never gets a chance to rest since you're always on guard, waiting for the next threat or injury. Over time, you may find you are constantly engaged in the same trauma response, as your brain has learned it is the only way to survive. For example, you may find you are a people pleaser at work, with your partner, with your friends, and even with your kids (fawn response), and you grew up with a narcissistic parent, or have a narcissistic wife at home. Or, you are aggressive, getting into arguments and fights with your family (fight response), on your commute, or in social situations, because as a child you were often beat up by your siblings or a parent, and learned the only way to survive was to become the aggressor.

If you are frequently experiencing one or more of these responses in the context of your relationship, this is your reality check: healthy, safe relationships should not trigger your body into trauma responses and chronic stress. Your body is speaking an eloquent, distinct, and clear message: **YOU ARE IN DANGER.**

The problem for most of us is that we don't recognize these reactions as trauma responses. When you are deeply entrenched in a trauma response pattern, the pain, the brain fog, the strong emotions, or perhaps the psychological numbness can make it feel nearly impossible to find-or fight- your way out of a relationship.

The chronic fawning response is particularly worrisome when you are in relationship with a narcissist, as you can become stuck in a perpetual cycle of trying to please someone who will never be satisfied with you. A narcissist can be triggered by anything and everything you do, and you may find yourself bending over backward to avoid the next argument or criticism. You will never make them happy, (nor should it ever be your job to make someone happy). Their abusive behavior, whether you're experiencing it in the moment, or simply anticipating their hideous antics, triggers you into a spiraling cycle of fawning. When you add the guilt and shame from the cognitive dissonance you're experiencing from the fawning behavior, you have a mountain of trauma building within you.

When you add the dynamics of gaslighting and blame shifting that are commonly used against you by a narcissist, you may get lodged into a spiral of fawning. The more you are gaslit or told you are the problem, the more your brain feels triggered into the fawning response (because it feels threatened), which leads to increased attempts to please and placate the narcissist. Since the prefrontal cortex, or rational part of your brain is off-line when you're experiencing threatening behavior, it becomes extremely challenging, if not impossible, to think clearly and find your way out of the toxic sludge of these relationships. This dynamic, along with cognitive dissonance, is what can keep a person trapped in these relationships for years.

Another aspect to consider about trauma is that it makes it very difficult to assess your intuition and "trust your gut" when your brain and body are chronically hijacked by these responses. The hypervigilance, anxious thinking, and emotional dysregulation become so "loud" that it can make your intuition impossible to hear. On the flipside, if you feel number and more disconnected from your body as a trauma response, you will also experience challenges in accessing intuitive messages.

Your body speaks your truth, and if it is speaking the language of trauma, it is begging you to find a way out of this relationship. It doesn't matter if this person doesn't meet the *DSM-5* criteria for narcissistic personality disorder, or if your friends think your partner is as kind as the Dalai Lama or as hot as Brad Pitt. You must learn to listen to your body's cues and trust them. This is all the information you need to know to help determine you are in an unhealthy relationship.

CHAPTER 8

THE LANGUAGE OF ATTACHMENT

Marielle had dreadlocks, tattoos of Hindu symbols covering her arms, and big brown eyes. She threw her shoes off, and folding her legs up onto the couch cushion, slumping her shoulders. She was a twenty-eight-year-old African American woman who came to me for therapy after experiencing conflict with her partner. Before she could mutter a few words, the tears streamed from her eyes. "I'm sorry. I guess my heart hurts," she cried.

She grew up in a home with an alcoholic, bipolar father who was a musician and artist. She described her dad as her best friend and shared the many ways he had influenced her spirituality and creativity. Her mother left them when she was five years old for another man, and Marielle hadn't seen her since. Only a handful of memories of her remained. Marielle knew her dad loved her, yet she shared memories of him disappearing for several days at a time, even when she was young. She'd be left to care for her two younger siblings. He would sometimes return with gifts and food, but never acknowledged he had disappeared. Sometimes he'd lay on the couch for days, so Marielle would cook, clean, and parent her siblings. She hoped that if she kept her dad happy, he wouldn't leave again. Marielle cherished his happy moods, as he would bring her into his studio to paint and play music and praised her artistic abilities. "I adore my dad. He's all I have."

Three years ago, Marielle met Sydney in her yoga studio. They fell in love quickly and moved in together within six months of dating. Sydney was a popular, well-respected yoga teacher and spiritual mentor to many in their community. Marielle described their relationship as "hot and cold," and described a pattern of intense fighting and reconciliation. Despite living together, Marielle feared Sydney wasn't committed to the relationship because Sydney often stayed at other women's homes overnight. When Marielle shared her concerns about Sydney not coming home at night, she was told she was "too fear based and jealous."

Since being with Sydney, Marielle recognized she had lost interest in creating art and music, as most of their time was focused on engaging in Sydney's yoga community and attending her classes and workshops. As tears fell from her eyes, Marielle said "I love her so much. She's this amazing human being who is so loving and inspiring to everyone. But sometimes I see this side of her that is so cruel. She tells me I'm stupid and makes me feel guilty for everything. I don't know if she even realizes how hurtful her comments are to me. She can fly into a rage for hours over the smallest things. I can't stand her when she's like that. But I know she's my soul mate and I can't imagine life without her."

Marielle said "I am really trying to let go of my ego so I can stop feeling so insecure, but every time she spends the night somewhere, I literally feel sick to my stomach. I don't sleep and all I can do is think about her cheating on me. When she comes back the next day, I am just completely shut down. I can't talk to her or even look at her, and sometimes I'll be mad for days. Sydney thinks I'm being overly dramatic and just leaves the house when I do this, which then makes me feel even worse."

Marielle had tried to break up with Sydney several times yet was consumed by thoughts that she'd never find another partner like Sydney. She sighed "I don't think anyone could love me as much as she has." Within days of each breakup, they would reconcile.

ATTACHMENT THEORY

Attachment theory deserves a place in this book, as in my clinical experience, it plays such a significant role in our relationships. It can be a source of protective resilience as well as vulnerability to a PLR. Depending on your attachment style, it can also be part of your red flag warning system. Essentially, attachment describes the bond between a child and its parent or caregiver that is developed in infancy and early childhood and is one of the most significant and pervasive influences on our personality, self-esteem, and relationships. The theory of attachment was developed by Dr. John Bowlby, a psychiatrist who theorized that children are born with biological programming to form attachments with others as a matter of survival (Bowlby, 1990).

As infants, we are given the basic guidance on what it means to be loved and how to trust others. A child's cries, smiles, coos, and eventually language stimulate a built-in caregiving response in adults. It is thought to be evolutionary in nature, as without this instinct to connect, humans may not survive as a species. It's important to note that attachment is not consciously controlled. It is hard wired into our nervous system and acts as a survival instinct. Essentially, we do not control this part of our brain. It controls us. Once our basic attachment style is wired into our brains in the first three to five years of life, most of us will remain consistent with it throughout our entire lives. However, attachment styles can be influenced in both positive and negative ways in adulthood (Levine and Heller, 2012).

There are complex ways to describe and understand attachment styles, but for simplicity's sake, we'll focus on four main attachment styles to give you a basic understanding of this theory and how it applies to PLRs. It is helpful to think of attachment styles on a spectrum, where a person can fall anywhere on the spectrum with varying degrees of each style.

Attachment theory assumes it is ideal for a child to be given the opportunity to form a healthy, secure attachment with a parent or caregiver (this does not have to be a biological parent) in the first few years of life. This secure attachment is formed when a parent responds consistently and lovingly to the child's needs over time. The child learns it is safe to express a need, and that it is safe to trust that others will respond to your needs and care for you. Essentially, relationships become a source of safety and comfort. This helps a child, and later, the adult, become confident in exploring the world and relationships.

If the attachment is disrupted by some kind of trauma, separation, or other challenging issues that can arise in childhood, there can be severe consequences throughout the entire lifespan. Examples could include the loss of a parent or caregiver through death, divorce, or other means, such as parental mental health or addiction issues, living in extreme poverty or a war zone, or other traumas. This disruption leads to one of the other three styles, avoidant, anxious, or disorganized. Here is a breakdown of the four main styles:

THE FOUR ATTACHMENT STYLES

SECURE
When children have the experience of love, acceptance, and nurturing in the early years, their brains become wired to expect more of this, developing a secure attachment style. I like to imagine the metaphor of a love buffet, where this child has a steady supply of love, and they trust that they will always be fed. Love is not scarce, it is abundant. Even when it is temporarily missing, it is just around the corner. Love is safe. It can be given, and it can also be received. Children with secure attachments grow into adults who tend to have more fulfilling, healthy, longer-term relationships. They tend to communicate their needs and emotions and have a healthy sense of trust in others and in themselves. Intimacy is not threatening, nor is independence. The securely attached person learns to love through interdependence with a partner.

AVOIDANT
Other children have the experience of experiencing very little love and attention, developing an avoidant attachment. If and when they are fed the leftovers of the love buffet, it is

just enough to survive. Their basic needs are met, but there is nothing interlaced with love, consistency, or nurturing. These infants instinctually express their needs to their caregivers by crying, cooing, or attempts at eye contact, yet the caregiver more often than not doesn't respond, delays their response, or meets the response with anger, irritability, or hostility. Eventually, these children stop expecting love, because it never came in the first place, or it came with pain. They were born with the instinct to ask for it, however the instinct is eventually extinguished when no one responds. They dutifully move through life alone, dependent on no one, since no one ever comes. No one is dependable. "No one is going to love me, so why try?" is their internal motto. It is not safe to be vulnerable and depend on others, so they do everything they can to avoid intimacy.

As adults, they tend to struggle with intimacy and commitment, and can be ultra-independent, as dependence is threatening. They also tend to struggle with identifying and expressing a broad range of emotions and can be somewhat disconnected from the internal cues of the body. They can sabotage relationships when they become more intimate by avoiding commitment, cheating, or finding fault in their partner.

DISORGANIZED

This style typically develops when the child or caregiver is experiencing severe abuse or neglect. Just like all infants, these children have the instinct to have their needs met by a caregiver. However, they have the unfortunate experience of experiencing fear in the moment their needs are met, or fear in place of having their needs met. They could have a mother who is traumatized, or living in fear, and every time this mother goes to nurture her child, the child feels two things: love coupled with the fear the parent is experiencing in the moment. This confusing experience becomes wired into the child's nervous system, essentially teaching the child that fear and love go hand in hand. As one might imagine, this can create paralyzing results in relationships. This is like walking up to the love buffet where a violent food fight is taking place. You never take a bite because you're too terrified to eat.

As adults, these types can have erratic patterns in relationship, sometimes vacillating between needing intense closeness yet pushing others away. They tend to have a sense of deep-rooted shame, feelings of inadequacy, and low self-worth. They usually have a deep fear of rejection and can struggle to connect with others. The difference between avoidant and disorganized people is that avoidants don't want intimacy and will try to avoid it. The disorganized type desires intimacy but will push it away out of fear. Many disorganized types will have PTSD or complex PTSD due to the trauma endured in childhood.

ANXIOUS

Marielle is an example of someone with an anxious attachment. What leads to an anxious attachment is the confusing experience of love being given freely, only to disappear at times. These children are constantly worried about love's dependability and predictability. They never feel a sense of security that love will stay. Their nervous systems become wired to remain on high alert to any sense that love will be taken away at any moment. They live a life where they are often willing to settle for the crumbs of connection, instead of asking for the full love buffet. Something is better than nothing, albeit unfulfilling or even dangerous at times.

The cognitive and emotional processes of someone with an anxious attachment have an uncanny knack for making them feel small, unworthy, and insignificant. They may feel like they are always maneuvering to maintain connection with anyone they're in a relationship with; friends, children, parents, partners, coworkers. They often feel like they will be too much for someone, or that they aren't enough. If they sense that someone is pulling away from them, they can become incredibly anxious and even go into something called protest behavior, which can look like they are pulling away or pushing a partner away, when really, they are begging for reconnection. Unfortunately, many anxiously attached people can be misdiagnosed with borderline or dependent personality disorder by mental health professionals who don't recognize this pattern.

IS YOUR ATTACHMENT STYLE MAKING YOU VULNERABLE?
In almost three decades of clinical work, I have witnessed survivors of PLRs with each attachment style. However, it has been my experience that there are significantly more clients who have had anxious or disorganized attachments who have fallen prey to pathological and narcissistic abuse. It isn't surprising, as both of these styles have qualities that can make a person particularly vulnerable to getting tangled in the web of abuse.

While securely attached individuals can certainly fall prey to a pathological partner, they can have some protective factors the other styles lack. Due to being more comfortable with intimacy and less triggered by fears of abandonment, they may be better equipped to set boundaries with a pathological partner's inappropriate behavior without fear of losing the relationship. They may communicate their needs and emotions more clearly, which could trigger anger or strong reactions in a pathological partner earlier in the relationship (therefore alerting them to the toxicity or danger of the partner), whereas other styles might struggle to be assertive and express clear needs and boundaries. They have likely experienced healthier role modeling of relationships in their past, so may be more aware of unhealthy relationship patterns to avoid.

ANXIOUS ATTACHMENT VULNERABILITIES
This particular attachment style makes people extremely vulnerable to narcissistic and pathological partners for a few reasons. In the beginning of a relationship with a narcissist, the mirroring and love-bombing can feel extremely soothing and fulfilling for the anxiously attached person, as they tend to struggle with low self-worth and feelings of inadequacy while craving connection and stability in their significant relationships. Since narcissists often begin relationships with heavy, frequent contact mixed with a desire to spend increased time with their targets, it can be especially difficult to convince someone with an anxious attachment to see this is a red flag. This is exactly what their mind, heart, and nervous system are wired to desire. Connection. Intimacy. Reassurance. Love. What feels like a dream to the anxiously attached person is actually a toxic, seductive drug that feeds their craving for love and safety.

Anxiously attached people are driven by the fear of abandonment, and will engage in fawning, fixing, and people pleasing to keep a person happy with them. When the anxious attachment system is engaged, dismissal and denial of the red flags strengthen in order to maintain the attachment (remember, this is a survival strategy and not necessarily conscious or rational). Essentially, the brain begins to bleach the red flags white. What also develops as the toxic partner's negative behaviors begin to surface are increased feelings and beliefs with themes of "I'm not good enough" and "I'm too much." This begins to tip the scales in the relationship as the anxiously attached person will idealize the narcissist while simultaneously devaluing themselves.

What does a narcissist love more than anything? Feeling admired, superior, and idealized by others. When you combine the anxiously attached person's fears of too muchness or not enoughness with the gaslighting, controlling, criticizing, and mindfuckery of the narcissist, it becomes a toxic combination that can keep the anxiously attached partner trapped in a vicious cycle of abuse. It is hard to question or challenge the putdowns when you already have a belief they are true.

Much like Marielle and Sydney, the hot and cold behavior of the narcissist keeps the anxiously attached person's nervous system in a state of hypervigilance, while experiencing the fawning trauma response. When the narcissist withdraws, gives the silent treatment, disappears unexpectedly, or in any way shows a behavior that feels threatening to the relationship, the anxiously attached person may become consumed with an overwhelming amount of anxiety and an instinct to reconnect with the partner. The distress can be so intense they may feel they can't focus on anything as they ruminate about what's happened to their partner, or what they did to create the distance. In this activated attachment state, you may even feel physical symptoms like nausea, a lack of appetite, insomnia, trembling, craving the partner, and in extreme cases, panic attacks. You may find yourself writing extensive text messages or providing detailed accounts of your feelings and thoughts to the partner in an attempt to reconnect. Your nervous system is craving a sign of reassurance and connection from the abandoning partner.

An anxiously attached person usually experiences a dynamic called protest behavior (Levine and Heller, 2012). This occurs when they've experienced the rejection or withdrawal of their attachment figure in significant ways, or for longer periods of time. What occurs is that their nervous system reaches a tipping point where they can no longer tolerate the anxiety of ambiguity or abandonment. When the person who disconnected from the anxiously attached person returns and attempts to reconnect, even though the anxiously attached person deeply needs and desires this reconnection, they end up pushing the partner away instead of moving toward the effort to reconnect. Protest behavior can look like withdrawal, pouting, acting cold or short with the offending person, and can also escalate into more significant behaviors such as leaving, threatening to break up, threatening suicide, or engaging in dramatic fights. This behavior, mixed with the narcissist's erratic and dramatic nature can create a volatile relationship riddled with fighting and arguing.

The nervous system is wired to attune to partners who continue to show you the same inconsistent patterns of love, attention, and safety you learned as a child. Even though you consciously desire someone who is dependable, safe, and consistent, you put up with the same patterns you've always known. When combined with the cognitive dissonance and trauma we've discussed previously, having an anxious attachment can lead to a dangerous entanglement in a toxic relationship. If you have an anxious attachment, and you are feeling the misery of what I've described here, this is your red flag that you are either in a relationship that is not compatible with your attachment style (at the very least), or in a pathological love relationship with a partner who is harming you.

AVOIDANT ATTACHMENT VULNERABILITIES

While the avoidant style can also be vulnerable to these relationships, they don't have the glue the anxious and disorganized style have. However, I have seen many avoidant people who had narcissistic or pathological parents. What can put them at risk is a tendency to be more disconnected from the physical, emotional, and social cues that could alert them to an unhealthy partner. Their childhood trauma and poor relationship role modeling from their past also creates risk. If you are unaware of your emotions or the sensations associated with fear or trauma, you don't have the internal radar system available to alert you to danger.

DISORGANIZED ATTACHMENT VULNERABILITIES

The disorganized style shares similar vulnerabilities as the anxiously attached person, as they can experience similar desires for connection, as well as the tendency to withdraw from others. However, their withdrawals are more often triggered by a fear of intimacy, and not so much as protest behavior. Since the disorganized type tends to have a history of trauma or complex PTSD, they may have a handicapped ability to discern red flags and to leave a relationship. Furthermore, it is likely a disorganized person has experienced relationship role modeling in abusive, chaotic, or fearful relationships. They may stay with a pathological person not because they like it, but because it is what they know. This is one of the most damaging combinations, as you are coming into a pathological love relationship with pre-existing trauma and will be met with more trauma. In my experience, these can be some of the most abusive relationships on the spectrum of domestic violence.

Attachment is an incredibly complex, powerful, influence on our relationships. This brief overview hardly does it justice. You may be surprised to learn just how much your style impacts your emotions, thoughts, behaviors, values, and your relationships, and as we've now learned, how much it can increase your vulnerability to pathological love relationships. The good news is, you can find support and healing for your attachment style through having a secure, healthy relationship, and/or by engaging in trauma and attachment focused psychotherapy.

CHAPTER 9

THE BODY SPEAKS YOUR TRUTH: THE LANGUAGE OF DISEASE

Sara, a thirty-eight-year-old financial adviser with perfectly straightened long blond hair sat on the edge of my couch. She straightened her back, carefully crossing one leg over the other. Despite her professional appearance, I noticed dark circles under her puffy eyes covered with heavy makeup. She carefully dotted her eyes with a tissue as she apologized, "I'm sorry. I don't know what's wrong with me. I don't even know why I'm here. I thought I was having a heart attack last week. I was driving home from work and had to pull over because I was nauseous, dizzy, and had chest pain. I panicked because I thought I was going to die, but the doctors in the emergency room ran every test in the book and told me there was nothing wrong. They referred me to you since they think I had a panic attack. I feel crazy. I really thought I was going to die."

As we explored her history, I learned Sara grew up with a narcissistic mother, and she described a series of unhealthy relationships she'd experienced since her early twenties. She had two young children and had been a single mother for several years, while working diligently to build her career. She met Thomas about two years ago.

"He's my soul mate. Even though we fight a lot, we always find our way back to each other" she proclaimed. "He can be the most sensitive, loving man. I never met someone who understands me the way he does."

Thomas had three children from a previous marriage, ages eight, six, and four. He shared parenting time with his ex-wife, so they often had a full house when all five children were there. He aspired to build his own construction business but had been working various jobs to supplement his income. Six months into their relationship, Sara allowed him to move in after he was fired and couldn't pay his rent.

She said "I understand how hard it is for him to take these jobs. He loves building homes and is so talented. He can't stand doing work that he isn't passionate about." She decided that allowing him to move in meant they were serious about the relationship. Thomas told her someday he would marry her and told her of how their lives would be so easy once his career became successful.

Sara described a chaotic household with five children, "well, sometimes I feel like I have six children, if you count Thomas. I've learned to be less of a perfectionist and just deal with a messy, loud house. His kids don't listen to a word I say. Going to work is my escape these days. But I come home and see he's been laying on the couch all day and he expects me to make dinner. He says he doesn't know how to cook so I have to make all of our meals, but it is honestly making me feel so resentful." Sara financially supported their family, worked a full-time job and took care of most of the household and parenting duties.

"He gets really angry sometimes, but he always apologizes. He's just under a lot of stress. I have asked him to help out with the bills and he tells me I'm being unsupportive and selfish, and love means taking care of your partner when they are down and out. I don't know. Maybe I am being too demanding" she said.

About a year prior to our first session, Sara said she began experiencing severe exhaustion along with chronic aches and pains, but doctors couldn't identify the cause. She also had IBS (irritable bowel syndrome) and had gained thirty pounds in two years. "I know I'm worn down. I have the worst insomnia. I just can't sleep. I wake up stressed about everything, or Thomas starts a fight right when I'm going to sleep and then I'm up all night. I feel like a zombie all day and can't focus or remember things. The doctors have tried everything. I take several medications for my stomach and pain, yet I still feel miserable."

THE BODY SPEAKS FOR US

Sara's story is a common scenario. I have seen countless clients over the years referred to my practice after having a serious panic attack, where they thought they were having a heart attack or dying. Anxiety and panic typically include physical sensations in the body which are often confusing, thought to be physical conditions such as a heart attack or a stomach ache. Many people have no idea that these sensations are mental health related, and simply ignore the symptoms or take medication without realizing the root cause. Not only did Sara experience a panic attack, but she was also experiencing IBS, pain, fatigue, and weight gain that notably developed after some time in the relationship with Thomas.

"When we have been prevented from learning how to say no, our bodies may end up saying it for us," states Dr. Gabor Maté in his 2003 book, *When the Body Says No: Exploring the Stress Disease Connection*. Sara's story is one of many examples of how our bodies speak to us through the language of illness, pain, and disease. This physical communication includes a spectrum of symptoms, from something mild or seemingly benign, like having tight shoulders after a tense day at work, to occasional diarrhea during stressful events, to tangible disease such as cancer, diabetes, or rheumatoid arthritis after chronic stress or trauma. In this chapter, we are going to explore the intricate language of the body and how it can alert us to danger and dysfunction in our relationships. There is ample research documenting the connection between disease and psychological symptoms and trauma. For example, these are common physical conditions and symptoms often diagnosed in people with PTSD:

- Diabetes
- Obesity
- Hypertension
- Stroke
- Arthritis

- Fibromyalgia
- Chronic fatigue
- Heart disease
- GI Issues: IBS (irritable bowel syndrome), Crohn's Disease, Colitis (McFarlane, 2010).

Other physical symptoms may include:

- **Panic attacks**: A panic attack is the abrupt onset of intense fear or discomfort that reaches a peak within minutes. Symptoms usually include at least four of the following: palpitations, pounding heart, or accelerated heart rate; sweating; trembling; shaking; sensations of shortness of breath or smothering also can occur.
- **Insomnia**: Difficulty falling or staying asleep. This is often connected to anxiety, depression, nightmares, or dysregulated hormones due to chronic stress.
- **Excessive fatigue**: Clearly this is a side effect of insomnia but can also be a general side effect from your adrenal system being fatigued and dysregulated.
- **Thyroid or adrenal problems**: These glands excrete hormones needed for metabolism. Too much or not enough of these hormones can lead to lethargy or too much energy.
- **Agitation:** Survivors are typically in a constant state of being angry or on high alert due to the unpredictable, stressful environment of being around the narcissist.
- **Feeling emotionally numb:** While this isn't necessarily a physical symptom, it is worthy of noting as some survivors disconnect from their bodies and emotions in order to avoid feeling any more pain. Therefore, feeling numb, or the lack of pain or discomfort when there should be pain is a symptom.

- **Abnormally high heart rate (tachycardia):** Stress can lead to a rapid heart rate.
- **High cholesterol:** Often related to poor eating habits, as it is hard to focus on healthy habits when faced with trauma.
- **Brain fog:** Survivors report feeling confused, foggy, unable to make decisions or concentrate, and having memory problems.
- **Pain or muscle tension:** Stress hormones keep the body in a tense, rigid state.
- **Irregular or cessation of menstrual cycles:** High stress affects our hormonal balance and can disrupt our cycle.
- **Weight gain around the belly:** Cortisol, a stress hormone, is stored in body fat, particularly around the belly region. People with chronic stress may struggle to lose weight.

If you are experiencing symptoms such as this, and have had a history of trauma, this is your body speaking to you. It is telling you that something is off, at the very least. The typical way of seeing this is to ask a doctor to diagnose a physical condition and treat it, usually with a lifestyle change (such as more exercise or healthy eating) or medication. Most western medical providers don't assess for deeper influences, such as psychological or emotional stress or trauma.

THE PHYSICAL EFFECTS OF CHRONIC STRESS

When you are experiencing chronic stress and trauma in a pathological love relationship, your body suffers as much as your mind and heart. Your brain and adrenal system are responsible for regulating stress responses. When these systems engage, our bodies experience a cascade of complex, interrelated reactions, affecting sleep, digestion, breathing, and heart rate, to name a few. It is hypothesized that our bodies were designed to endure short periods of stress or threat solely for the purpose of survival when earlier human beings lived in less developed civilizations. Ideally, we are meant to react only in moments of acute stress, such as surviving a dangerous situation, doing something wildly exciting like riding a roller coaster or giving a speech. Yet in today's world, many situations create prolonged periods of intense stress, triggering a constant release of stress hormones such as cortisol and adrenaline. In these conditions, it is likely the body will experience harm and possibly permanent damage (Maté, 2003).

The endless flow of stress hormones and their effects on the body create inflammation, increasing your risk for a multitude of diseases, chronic pain, and other symptoms. Inflammation is good in small doses, as it helps our bodies fight disease and heal. However, stress induced chronic inflammation has the opposite effect. Emerging research shows many symptoms and diseases are rooted in stress and trauma, yet this concept is widely unrecognized by most western medical and mental health professionals.

Due to this paradigm, many of us are fairly unaware of the connection between the stress in our lives and the symptoms in our bodies. We live in a culture that encourages us to medicate our aches, sorrows and symptoms away without digging deeper. We alleviate the symptoms instead of addressing the root cause of disease. With electronics, medication, substance abuse, a constant bombardment of stimulation and *all-the-things*, along with our busy modern world, we have become disconnected from the most primitive, simple, and accurate source of information, the body.

In my interviews with survivors and in my clinical and personal experience, most PLR survivors present with at least one or more physical symptoms as listed previously. There is a plethora of studies about the connection between stress, trauma, and illness. In particular, research has shown an association between women with a history of intimate partner violence, (which could also be considered a pathological love relationship), and an increased development of autoimmune diseases such as fibromyalgia and chronic fatigue syndrome (Chandan, et.al., 2019).

Another study found that women who had experienced physical or sexual abuse, whether it first occurred as children or adults, "had more pain, non-GI somatic symptoms, bed disability days, lifetime surgeries, psychological distress, and functional disability compared to those without abuse histories." Rape and life-threatening physical abuse had the worst outcomes (Leserman, et.al., 1996).

Traditionally, the brain and nervous system took all the credit for engineering and running the intricate systems of our bodies. However, we now know the gut, which contains around one hundred million nerve cells (even more than the spinal column) actually sends signals to the brain. This is why Dr. Michael D. Gershon, author of the 1999 book, *The Second Brain: A Groundbreaking New Understanding of Nervous Disorders of the Stomach and Intestine,* coined the term "the second brain" to explain the gut is as powerful as the brain in regulating and directing the body. The gut is highly responsive to emotional stimuli, and if triggered, can immediately send its entire blood supply throughout the body to supply the limbs or organs with the fuel needed to respond to a threat.

Dr. Gabor Maté explains the powerful communication between brain and gut as such: the brain sends information to the gut from sensory organs (such as the eyes, skin, ears) after interpreting the data by the brain's emotional centers. The gut reinforces the emotional interpretation of the information, sending signals back to the brain. This dynamic creates the "gut feeling" we consciously understand. This gut-brain communication is vital to help us know whether our environment is safe.

Research also demonstrates the damaging effects of emotional trauma on the brain. Psychologist Dr. Daniel Goleman, author of *Emotional Intelligence: Why It Can Matter More Than IQ (2005)*, shares that emotional trauma can shrink the hippocampus, which is the part of the brain that is responsible for learning and memory. At the same time, the amygdala, which is responsible for more primitive emotions and survival instincts such as fight/flight, shame, guilt, envy, fear, and grief, becomes enlarged. According to Goleman, everything we learn, do, read, understand, and experience is dependent on the hippocampus functioning correctly.

What does this mean for survivors of a PLR? The part of your brain that helps you remember and learn new things decreases in size and function, and your ability to regulate and experience healthy emotional responses can be impacted. An overactive amygdala can lead to symptoms of PTSD. As you can imagine, the longer you stay in an abusive or toxic relationship, the harder it will become for you to function at your highest capacity.

STOP BEING SO NICE. IT'S KILLING YOU.

In his 2003 book, *When the Body Says No: Exploring the Stress Disease Connection*, Dr. Gabor Maté states, "we no longer sense what is happening in our bodies and cannot therefore act in self-preserving ways. The physiology of stress eats away at our bodies not because it has outlived its usefulness but because we may no longer have the competence to recognize its signals." As a Canadian physician respected for his expertise in trauma, addiction, and childhood development, Maté has challenged today's traditional western medicine approach that views the body and mind as separate from each other. His work is inspired by the field of psychoneuroimmunology, which is the study of the interaction between the mind and emotions, their interaction with the nervous system, and how both of them are intricately linked to our immune system. Maté documented substantial research indicating a connection between stress, trauma, emotion, and disease in his book, as he highlights trauma and emotional patterns commonly seen in people with certain diseases.

Among many examples Maté shared in his book is one of particular interest for PLR survivors. The medical community has noticed patients with ALS, or Lou Gehrig's Disease, almost always have a "nice," agreeable, accommodating personality. Typically, these patients tend to have histories of childhood loss or emotional deprivation. As adults they resist help and support from others, tend to be very driven, and deny or dismiss emotional and physical pain.

This immediately piqued my interest as a therapist who works with attachment, trauma, and PLRs. These traits could also be used to describe someone who experiences a chronic fawning response, an anxious attachment, or the personality super traits of many PLR survivors. Indeed, upon further research, I found a 2018 study showing female ALS patients have three personality traits in common... **agreeableness, conscientiousness**, and **extraversion** (Parkin Kullmann, Hayes, and Pamphlett, 2018). Now if you recall, agreeableness and conscientiousness happen to be the two super traits that are also common in PLR survivors. There's more.

Let's talk breast cancer. Maté also shared the following: "Research has suggested for decades that women are more prone to develop breast cancer if their childhoods were characterized by emotional disconnection from their parents or other disturbances in their upbringing; if they tend to repress emotions; particularly anger; if they lack nurturing social relationships in adulthood; and if they are the altruistic, compulsively caregiving types." Again, "altruistic, compulsively caregiving type" sounds hauntingly familiar to PLR survivors, and if you add the abuse of your primary relationship, you may also experience the absence of your "nurturing social relationships."

Furthermore, most of you are familiar with the concept of a "Type A" or "Type B" personality, whereas Type A is more aggressive, impatient, and controlling, and Type B is more balanced and displays healthy emotional expression. There is also a growing idea of a "Type C" personality that displays a combination of traits often found in people who develop cancer. These include patience, passivity, being more accepting and cooperative, and lacking assertiveness. Type C people tend to repress or suppress emotion, in particular, anger, while attempting to appear happy (Maté, 2003). Are you noticing a trend here?

Now let me be clear. I am not sharing this to frighten those of you with super traits, an anxious attachment, or trauma. If anything, these findings present more questions than answers, and highlight the need for more research in the field of PLRs and the mind-body connection. I share this because I want to highlight the risks presented in exposing yourself to long-term trauma and stress.

These examples are only a few of many that Maté and other researchers have found that highlight this idea that there are particular personality types and emotional response patterns that correlate with disease and illness. It is important to note that most of this research tends to point toward the repression or suppression of emotion in these personality types, more than the personality type itself. For example, being agreeable and nice to everyone you meet is not leading to disease. However, if you were an agreeable person, but held a lot of anger and resentment because you felt you were always giving and never receiving from others, yet didn't express this resentment, you could be at risk for disease. Clearly there is more to learn in this area, nonetheless this information can provide an opportunity to self-reflect and nurture your connection between mind, body, and emotion.

LISTENING TO THE BODY: INTEROCEPTION

Interoception is defined as a conscious or unconscious awareness of the internal signals in the body. It explains how our bodies register cues, such as a grumbling in our stomach that sends a signal to our brain that we are hungry, which creates the thought *I'm hungry, I need to eat lunch.* By listening to the cues of our body (whether we are conscious of it or not), we do *everything*. We eat when we are hungry. We sleep when we are tired. We reach out to a friend when we need connection. Sensations from the body also lead to our emotional feelings, especially those that are intense, or survival based, such as fear. Without interoceptive awareness, we would be unable to identify, understand, and respond appropriately to the signals in our body (Craig, 2015).

In his 2015 book, *The Body Keeps the Score: Brain, Mind, and Body in the Healing of Trauma*, Bessel van der Kolk states, "neuroscience research shows that the only way we can change the way we feel is by becoming aware of our inner experience and learning to befriend what is going on inside of ourselves." One of the benefits of increased interoceptive awareness is an increased ability to recognize physical cues that lead to emotional responses, which can then lead to the ability to prepare for and understand the responses better. Basically, we need interoceptive awareness to interpret our internal and external environments which in turn helps us manage emotional reactions.

For example, you may recognize that your heart is beating faster than normal and instead of thinking you might be having a heart attack, you realize that you are simply anxious because you are about to give a speech. When we don't recognize or understand the physical sensations in our bodies, it can lead to more discomfort, confusion, and a decreased lack of tolerance for the sensation or resulting emotion. When we know what we are feeling, why we are feeling it, and notice that all of the sensations change in time, it can help us cope and manage difficult emotions and situations more effectively.

The problem is trauma decreases our interoceptive abilities. Research shows ongoing trauma reduces our interoceptive awareness, meaning that people who experience chronic stress or trauma may have a difficult time receiving or interpreting messages from the body that help them understand the environment around them. People who have had adverse childhood events or trauma tend to have lower interoceptive awareness which leads to higher rates of PTSD. People with higher interoceptive awareness tend to have lower rates of PTSD. Why is this?

Research repeatedly indicates that people who experience chronic stress or trauma begin to experience a "buffering" effect in their nervous system. Essentially, their interoceptive awareness is turned down in the body's effort to protect itself from the intense, ongoing effects of stress. This leads to a decreased ability to listen to the body's cues, and therefore to respond appropriately to them. People may experience hypersensitivity and heightened emotional reactivity, or under-reaction and decreased sensitivity to the body's cues. This buffering can remain intact long after the need for protection has passed, potentially causing long-term difficulties in understanding and coping with the body's cues which lead to emotional responses and decision-making (Price and Hooven, 2018). In contrast, a nurturing environment with a relatively "normal" level of stress can help you be in tune with your body's sensations and may help you cope with stress more easily (Del Giudice, et al., 2011).

WHY WE MUST LISTEN TO THE BODY

Here's the takeaway. If we are not able to notice or interpret the cues in our bodies, especially when the body is giving us signals that we are in danger, we may not realize the danger, threat, or dysfunction around us. It is crucial to increase our interoceptive awareness so we can utilize the gift of our bodies to help us navigate through our relationships. People who come into a PLR with histories of trauma and lower interoceptive awareness may find it more difficult to "trust their gut" about a relationship, as the lines of communication between the gut and brain are diminished or difficult to interpret. For those of you who have higher degrees of interoceptive awareness may experience a decreased ability over time as you are exposed to the trauma of a PLR, further diminishing your ability to "trust to your gut" about the relationship. Your body is a powerful source of information if the lines of communication are open. Fortunately, there are ways to increase your interoceptive awareness, which we will explore later in this book.

Hopefully you are starting to understand why it is so important to master the language of your physical body, and the cues it provides in helping you identify whether you are in a toxic relationship. Your body can be the messenger to tell you that something is wrong. If you are dealing with a narcissist or toxic person, you have likely been manipulated, lied to, and gaslit so much that you start to doubt yourself and your reality. Not only do they use these tactics to disorient you and make you feel crazy and dependent on them, but your brain may also be experiencing additional challenges due to the effects of stress on the hippocampus. If you are feeling like a dazed and confused crazy person, this is why!

We've also learned there can be serious effects on your health, especially when you're exposed to these toxic relationships over longer periods of time. You must ask yourself if this narcissist is worth your physical, mental, and emotional health. Even if you feel like you can't take a step forward yet, it is important to acknowledge the damage that this relationship can do to your health.

Remember there are two ways to help yourself identify and cope with a toxic relationship. One is external, which is what most people do when they realize that something is off. This involves doing your research, whether it is by using the internet, reading books, or talking to friends or a therapist to help you understand. This external method will help you orient to a healthier reality and can decrease your self-doubt and increase your support system which is crucial to surviving these relationships. However, the internal method of developing a relationship with your body and becoming fluent in its language is equally, if not more important, for your own body is more accurate than any therapist, book, Google article, or friend's opinion in alerting you to the danger in your life.

PART THREE

EMPOWERED ACTION

CHAPTER 10

HEALING: THE FIRST STEPS

―

Broken. This is how many survivors feel after enduring the horrendous abuse of a pathological love relationship. I know I did. You may feel like you've lost yourself- your mental, emotional, physical, and spiritual health. Feel like a walking zombie? Yeah, that's common too, especially if you are still in the relationship, or have recently left. At some point you may believe that you've moved on, but as soon as you attempt to date again, you realize that trusting another person with your heart is nearly impossible. Some of you may decide you'll never take a chance on love again.

There's hope, I promise. You can heal this, and believe it or not, you can learn to trust in yourself and in love again. Have you ever heard of Kintsugi? It is an ancient Japanese art form, which consists of taking broken objects, such as a ceramic cup or plate, and binding the pieces back together with gold or silver glue. Instead of disposing of the broken object or trying to hide the breakage, it essentially highlights the scars as they become part of a beautiful piece of art.

Kintsugi can serve as a powerful metaphor as you recover from the heartbreak of a toxic relationship. You may feel broken, unsure of yourself, and for some, even hopeless to find healing, yet in the process of healing, you may find that you are more beautiful, resilient, and unique than you ever could have imagined. It may feel like a stretch, but it could even be possible that your scars are transformed into something more beautiful as you integrate the learning and growth opportunities that are possible from loss and trauma.

Photo: Marco Montalti

STOP SHOULD-ING ON YOURSELF

Before we discuss specifics on how to begin your healing journey, it is important to understand a few things about healing from trauma. First of all, remember healing is a process, not a destination. I encourage you to start with a huge dose of patience and compassion for yourself and this journey. If you are reading this book, you have already begun your healing process, as you are increasing your awareness of this issue. Some of you may be completely out of your partner's life by this point and have already done some therapy or other forms of healing. Some of you may have just started to question whether you are dealing with a narcissist or toxic partner, and you have no idea where to start.

Recovering from a pathological love relationship can be lengthy and complex, varying for everyone. People can struggle for years, if not their entire lives (without treatment) and may even feel shame or confusion about why they can't "get over it." Remember that a significant portion of a pathological love relationship is psychological and emotional abuse. These are invisible wounds that destroy your self-worth, your identity, your ability to trust yourself and others. Your body also suffers from ongoing trauma and stress and may require its own healing process. It takes work to heal the deepest wounds to the psyche, body, heart, and spirit. This often presents a challenge, because without support and feedback with a therapist or helping professional, you may not even realize the way you feel about yourself, the self-doubt, lack of confidence, or self-destructive relationship patterns you may have developed is connected to the destructive psychological abuse you experienced.

We are all unique, and our perceptions of trauma are highly subjective. One thing I often hear from trauma survivors is "what happened to me it isn't as bad as…." (Insert someone else's horrific trauma experience here). Please understand trauma is in the eye of the beholder. Two people may experience the exact same traumatic event but will have very different reactions to the event. It is common for survivors to dismiss and minimize bad things that happened to them, which can be a form of denial and avoidance of the pain or connected to cognitive dissonance. It can also be rooted in core beliefs of inadequacy, where you feel like you're not good enough nor are you worthy of love, healing, attention, etc. Some may still feel responsible for aspects of the abuse, which is common after experiencing narcissistic gaslighting.

Please stop *should-ing* on yourself. You have been a victim of abuse, and you have every right to be suffering from this experience. There is no shame in being right here, right now. Should-ing on yourself sounds like:

"It's been years! I *should* be feeling better by now, but I can't stop thinking about him!" or,

"It wasn't that bad. I *shouldn't* be so upset about it" or,

"I *should* be able to move on."

Even if you aren't should-ing on yourself, you may hear those types of statements from friends and family who may care deeply about you, but likely have no idea of the depth and complexity of the trauma you've experienced. Don't let others who have not walked in your shoes define how you should or should not be feeling.

Your experience is unique to you, and a myriad of factors can sometimes lead to a longer recovery, including the following:

- The length of time you were involved with the pathological partner
- The severity of the abuse (meaning, your perception of the severity of the abuse)
- Whether you experienced one traumatic event or years of chronic abuse
- A history of childhood trauma, PTSD, or complex PTSD
- Safety, legal, social, economic, cultural, gender, religious, or other barriers that make it difficult to leave the relationship (i.e., threats of harm, legal issues from a divorce or fight for parenting time, financial dependence, sharing children, lack of employment or job skills that limit your ability to be self-sufficient, religious or cultural rules, etc.)
- Other factors that keep you in survival mode and unable to focus on recovery

START WHERE YOU ARE

Healing is cyclical, not linear. It can be messy, painful, and somedays you may feel like you've taken the proverbial two steps forward, one step back, or one step forward, two steps back. There were some days where I thought I would never escape my relationship, or the black hole of grief, despair, and pain that I felt. However, I found my way out, and have seen countless clients and friends in my life find their way out too. Have faith in yourself. You can do this.

What does it mean to start where you are? Each of you have different circumstances and relationships with the abuser in your life. I often have people come to me in therapy who say they want to begin trauma work, but they are still living with their pathological partner and being abused on a daily basis. Trauma work happens in layers, with the initial step being the creation of safety. Ideally, a therapist skilled in trauma treatment and pathological love relationships can help you navigate your way through this process.

The first step is to prioritize your needs. To do this, I'm going to introduce you to *Maslow's Hierarchy of Needs*, developed by psychologist and founder of Humanistic Psychology, Dr. Abraham Maslow. In his 1997 book, *Motivation and Personality*, he shared his theory that people must have certain basic needs met in life before they can pursue emotional, social and higher-level needs he called "self-actualization."

Some basic takeaways to help you understand this model:

- Humans are motivated by this hierarchy of needs
- The order of these needs is not linear
- This may vary based on the individual and life circumstances
- Most of us will be motivated by more than one of these needs at a time
- These needs are organized by necessity, meaning ideally, one or more of the basic needs must be met to get to the higher needs
- However, one can still meet higher-level needs without having the lower-level needs met

Essentially, Maslow's idea was we must first have basic needs met in order to be able to focus on higher-level needs. For example, if you are starving, and have no safe place to live, you are likely not going to be exerting your energy or focus on improving your self-esteem or personal growth. You're going to be focused on finding food and shelter. It is not to say that someone may not be thinking of those other needs, however they will not be your primary driving force.

For the purposes of this book, I want to use this hierarchy only as an inspiration, as there are many problems with this basic model that make it inappropriate to lean on due to insufficient data regarding socioeconomic, cultural, gender, and other influences that weren't widely considered in the 1940s. Fortunately, researchers have expanded upon this model over the years, and continue to find ways to understand and implement it into our modern world that is more inclusive of the factors mentioned above. There is more understanding that this model is not linear and can be cyclical and multifaceted. People may find themselves moving back and forth to fulfill different needs based on life circumstances.

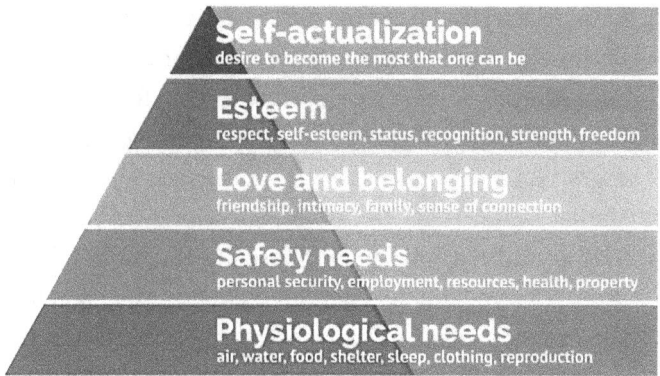

1. **Physiological needs:** These are your basic survival needs, such as food, drink, air, shelter, sleep, clothing, sex. These are the most fundamental needs to keep us alive and

functioning optimally. Maslow believed these needs must be met before any other needs can be met.
2. **Safety needs:** We need to feel a sense of structure, predictability, and control in our lives. Living in a society with laws, medical care, and other resources that help us feel secure are part of this. Examples include having social stability, financial security (by government resources, employment, or other means), laws to keep citizens safe, medical care and resources. This also includes a general need of feeling free from fear, which is an important consideration for those experiencing PLRs.
3. **Love and belongingness needs:** A feeling of belongingness is fundamental and cross cultural. Belongingness means that you have a need for being connected to others through interpersonal relationships or affiliation with a group. This includes relationships, friendships, and the aspects of intimacy, love, trust, and affection.
4. **Esteem needs:** These include our feelings of accomplishment, self-worth, and respect. This can be internal and external, in that we can have esteem for ourselves (achievement, feeling good at something, integrity, dignity), or we can seek it from others (privilege and status).
5. **Self-actualization needs:** These are the highest level and are connected to a person feeling they've reached their highest potential or are engaged in building this over time. This may include personal growth and experiencing peak experiences. This is an overall desire to be all you can be. Examples could be attaining your goals as an athlete or artist, or reaching economic, career, spiritual growth, or parenting goals (Maslow, 1997).

HOW TO APPLY MASLOW'S HIERARCHY TO YOUR LIFE

Your healing journey will have many layers to it. This model can help you identify where to start if you are unsure of where to focus. At any and every stage of this model, it is helpful and recommended to seek help with a therapist or professional who is experienced in working with pathological love relationship recovery. Depending on where you are on the hierarchy, the professional help may vary. For example, if you are in immediate, physical danger, you need to turn to law enforcement or a domestic violence shelter in order to meet your safety needs. If you are not in immediate danger, and your basic needs are met, you may be in a better position to seek therapy or use other resources (books, YouTube, etc. if cost or availability of treatment is limited) to begin your healing journey.

PHYSIOLOGICAL AND SAFETY NEEDS

If you are being physically or sexually abused, or having basic needs threatened, such as being denied food, appropriate shelter, medical care, or money to meet basic needs, your survival and safety are most important. What can you do in these situations? You must first ask yourself, what are the fundamental needs that must be met in order for me to leave, or find the courage to leave? You need food, shelter, and other basic living needs, along with some semblance of safety and security.

Here are some primary guidelines and ideas for you if you are living with a narcissistic partner:

- If you are in immediate danger, call 911 or leave if you can.
- If the danger is not immediate, develop an escape plan.

- Your escape plan should include gathering important documents and access to financial resources, such as IDs, birth certificates, and social security cards for you or dependents if you have them, health insurance, financial or legal information, etc. Keep these copies in a safe place outside of your home if possible, or hidden where you can have quick, easy access.
- Be prepared to change PINs, logins, and access to bank and all internet accounts in your name if you leave.
- If possible, try to have some cash on hand you can take with you for emergencies.
- Identify helpers and resources. Do you have a trusted friend, colleague, or family member who you confide in? Can they offer you a safe place to stay, even if temporary?
- Know about domestic violence resources in your area. Most will have websites with helpful information and can direct you to a safehouse if you need shelter.
- You may be able to obtain a protection or restraining order, which is a legal document that prevents the abuser from having contact with you. You can contact your local courthouse, domestic violence hotline, or police for information on how to get one.
- Most importantly, but also very challenging for many: DO NOT RETURN TO OR CONTACT the abuser if at all possible. Breaking free can be very difficult due to many factors. Remember, it takes an average of seven attempts to leave an abuser before a survivor permanently leaves the relationship.

If you are fearing for your safety or your life, no matter what your partner says, you must develop a plan to leave. If you've learned anything from this book, hopefully you now know why leaving is so hard. **Please hear this: Not once in my entire career have I ever worked with a survivor who actually had the experience of a highly pathological partner getting better or changing their ways. Not once.**

What often changes are their actions and words for a short time, which will last just long enough to pull you back in. They will usually try to sweet talk you back in and smother you with apologies and promises to never hurt you again. They may gaslight you into believing you are the problem, and that their abuse was your fault, such as "you know I had a stressful day. If you wouldn't have asked me to do the dishes, I wouldn't have lost my temper." Or they may manipulate and threaten you if you don't return.

This is the most crucial time to tune in to your body and LISTEN so you don't fall into the trap and be swayed by cognitive dissonance, trauma, or attachment anxiety. Your mind will likely start spinning with anxiety and confusion. You may feel sadness, loss, and anticipate life without your partner. You may have thoughts of scarcity and inadequacy, such as: *There's no one else who will love me. He's the only one who would put up with me. There is no one else like her. It's too hard to leave because I will lose.... (money, housing, etc.). He was my soul mate.* You may find your mind idealizing them and finding all the things you loved about them. You may also feel fear of what they will do to you if you leave. This can be overwhelming, especially if you've been threatened, if you are married, have children together, share finances, have no financial or housing resources, or are completely isolated from others. If this is the case, this is where Maslow's Hierarchy can be useful.

REMEMBER THAT THE ABSENCE OF FEAR IS PART OF THESE SAFETY NEEDS.

You may be in a relationship with a narcissist who has never physically hurt you. However, the verbal, psychological, and emotional abuse is just as significant, if not more. This is another reason that leaving is important. When you are living in a state of real or perceived threat and danger, your nervous system will not be able to relax and find energy to focus on these higher-level goals. Again, listening to the signals your body is giving you can guide you into knowing whether you need to leave the situation or relationship.

LOVE AND BELONGINGNESS NEEDS

If your basic physiological and safety needs are met, or mostly met, then you may be in a more stable place to begin more consistent therapy or even trauma treatment, depending on your situation and available resources. In this stage of the model, there can be some challenges. As humans, we have a core need to belong, which may tempt you into staying with your partner. You may fear losing your family or friends if you leave as well. It is also common for pathological partners to keep you isolated, so you may feel like you have no friends or family to turn to if you do leave.

If you find you need some tender loving care in this stage, it might be helpful to do the following:

- Identify **trusted** friends or family, who believe you and will not report back to your partner.
- Explore private Facebook groups you can join to find free support and validation. (You can join my Facebook group: Toxic Relationship Recovery).

- If you have the financial or healthcare resources available, find a therapist who is trained and experienced in treating trauma and pathological love relationships.
- Look for Meetup or local groups that focus on this topic.
- Most importantly, begin to develop a self-care routine to begin treating yourself with love and respect. The relationship with yourself is of primary importance after all.
- Try to rekindle relationships with friends who you may have lost contact with during your relationship. Authenticity can be helpful. You can say something like "I'm really sorry if I neglected our friendship while I was with… I have been struggling and discovered that he was a narcissist. Part of the abuse I have been through was him trying to keep me isolated from family and friends. I am trying to heal and need to rebuild my friendships. Can you forgive me? I really miss you and want to be a better friend."

The point here is to build a community of support around you, even if it is one person, one professional, or one Facebook group to begin with. Your goal is to decrease your reliance on the pathological partner for love and belongingness needs and find others who can meet this need for you.

ESTEEM NEEDS

This level is vital to your recovery. It can take a lot of time to rebuild due to the psychological and emotional abuse you've suffered. It might be helpful to identify even the smallest things you have done that highlight your resilience and strength. If you have made it this far, you are a survivor. You have more strength than your partner will ever have. Your body, your heart, your mind, and spirit have learned unbelievable coping mechanisms in order to support your survival. You may not believe this, because you may feel worthless, unlovable, and struggling with low self-confidence due to the messages you've heard over time. But they are just that- *messages*. They are not truth. You must learn to discern between your partner's toxic abuse and your truth.

This area is a place to insert a heavy dose of compassion for yourself and your choices. Remember being abused by a narcissist or toxic partner is not your fault. I don't care if someone has labeled your choices or behaviors as codependent, or if they are somehow blaming you for this abuse. ABUSE IS ABUSE. Hopefully by now you've learned there are so many factors contributing to your involvement in these toxic relationships. *No one ever consciously chooses to be loved by a toxic person.*

Here are some ideas to help you begin to build your esteem needs:

- Make a list of all of the ways you have been strong or resilient in your life or in this relationship.
- Identify things that are going well in your life, even if it is a small step, like, you took a shower today!
- If you are free from your partner, begin taking steps to get to know and cherish yourself again. This could include a focus on a hobby, caring for your body with nourishing food, rest, exercise, or meditation.
- Work with a therapist to help you heal the layers of psychological and emotional trauma.
- Get in touch with your inner child. What messages do they need to hear to build their self-esteem?

YOUR SELF-ACTUALIZATION NEEDS

This step may come later in your healing, after other needs have been addressed and you have the energy, time, and internal or external resources to focus on this area. These needs typically center around reaching your fullest potential as a human. They often encompass things like seeking mystical spiritual experiences, a deep connection with nature, or aspirational career or service goals. It can also mean becoming more vulnerable and authentic, as you work through layers of shame and become more self-accepting.

While Maslow placed this at the top of his hierarchy, I believe that this level, along with some of the others, can be experienced without the other needs being met. In fact, some of these experiences can actually catapult your healing. For example, if you are a spiritual person and seek meditative, energetic, or other spiritual healing methods, you may find that these experiences help you make decisions or have healing insights that move you forward in your journey faster than psychotherapy. It is important to note that meeting self-actualization needs does not mean that your life is perfect, and you become free from challenges. It might mean that you handle challenges with more ease and grace, more optimistic perspectives, or with a stronger sense of resiliency. Self-actualization is an ongoing process, and not a final destination.

Some characteristics and qualities of self-actualized people include:

- Spontaneity.
- Creativity.

- Search for peak experiences which are moments of joy, euphoria, and wonder. These could be mystical, spiritual through personal growth, or simply a beautiful moment in nature or watching children playing.
- Have a strong sense of justice and concern for the good of all.
- Are more comfortable with the unknown.
- Have compassion and acceptance for people and their differences.

Overall, I want you to remember these basics. Healing takes time, and each person's journey is unique. Try to avoid comparing yourself to others or judging yourself for your progress. These are invisible wounds you're dealing with, so if recovery feels like an uphill battle, this is why. There are many stages to your recovery, and you may find yourself all over the place as you sort your way through this. That is perfectly normal and to be expected. This can be messy, confusing, and incredibly painful. But it is possible. Have faith in your resilience and know that if you are reading this, you are on the right track. You may feel broken, yet just like a piece of Kintsugi, one day you will hopefully see the beauty in your scars.

CHAPTER 11

HOW TO LISTEN

We've covered a lot of ground so far. You've learned about the traits to help you identify a narcissist, sociopath, or toxic person. We've learned about factors that can make you more vulnerable to a pathological love relationship. We've covered some of the important internal red flags and vulnerabilities, such as trauma responses, illness and disease, and your attachment style.

The question is, how do you put all of this knowledge together so you can apply it to your life and relationships? In order to become toxic love proof, you must hone your internal and external radar so you can identify, interpret, and act upon the red flags of a relationship. This becomes challenging when you have likely been taught not to listen to yourself and to distrust your reality. But somewhere deep inside, the truth is there, even if it is just a whisper.

One of the benefits of turning inward and honoring your internal radar system is it frees you from having to judge, diagnose, or condemn someone else. The only person you have to be concerned with is you. If YOU don't feel good about something, then that is your "problem" to solve, not theirs. This is the ultimate form of taking responsibility for yourself. You get to choose who is allowed into your life and who is not. This is true empowerment. While we may have been victims of abuse, we are ultimately responsible for our choices and actions.

Are you ready to make a commitment to yourself? Are you ready to turn the compassion inward and focus the love on the one who truly needs it? If so, I want to introduce you to my **LISTEN** strategy that can help you learn to tune in to your magical body, mind, heart, and intuition so they can guide you toward safety, self-love, and healthy, loving relationships with yourself and others.

THE LISTEN STRATEGY:
Listen With Intention
Insight
Sanctuary
Translate and **T**rust
Empowered Action
Nurture and Heal

LISTEN WITH INTENTION
Let's consider the word *listen*. Hearing and listening are two different things, right? It is one thing to simply notice, see, hear, or feel the red flags of a relationship, but that means nothing if there is no intention behind it. It is important to notice the red flags, however, you must take it one step further, which is to actually *LISTEN*. Listening is an active process which includes the intention of purposefully integrating the information you "hear." Listening means nothing if you

lack the intention to stay open and curious to the information you receive. Unfortunately, we avoid listening to the truth because of influences such as cognitive dissonance, trauma, or your attachment style. We may also be more attached to the outcome of the relationship than we are to our own safety or sanity. When you're attached to the outcome, your thoughts may sound something like this:

- This is your soul mate, and you just can't imagine life without them.
- You were supposed to get married to Prince Charming, have two kids, the house, the life…and you believe you have it (except for the fact that you're being abused).
- You're thirty, your biological clock is ticking, and you don't want to lose your chance of having a child, so you stay.
- You can't stand the idea of being divorced or single.
- You've spent decades together and the thought of starting over paralyzes you.
- You fear financial instability or ruin if you leave.
- Religious or cultural beliefs make it seem impossible to leave.
- You experience thoughts of love scarcity, such as *no one else will love me like this, I won't find another person with their qualities, etc.*

Listening requires paying attention to both external and internal red flags. You can continue to educate yourself about the signs of pathology, such as narcissism, sociopathy, and psychopathy as you notice the behaviors of your partner that concern or confuse you. You must also listen to your internal red flags as we've identified in this book. But then what?

The Yamabushi monks in Japan practice a philosophy called *uketamo*, which loosely translates to "I humbly accept with an open heart" (Itani, 2021). Buddhist philosophy also teaches the art of acceptance as a practice to reduce suffering. Listening with intention means accepting *what is*. You must become an objective witness to your reality, an observer, a seer of truth. You don't judge or dismiss it; you simply notice it. You remove your blinders and stop seeing what you want to see. Can this be extremely challenging? Absolutely. As we've learned, this is difficult for many reasons, especially if you are experiencing cognitive dissonance, have an anxious attachment, super traits, or trauma that has influenced your perceptions and reactions.

With acceptance also comes surrender. To let go of that which you lack control over is terrifying but freeing. When you can accept that your partner is a narcissist, an abuser, or simply someone who is hurting you, it frees you to take action. Of course, cognitive dissonance can make it difficult to land on a place of acceptance of what is yet creating a mindset that embraces acceptance and surrender is one step toward reducing the dissonance. Some powerful resiliency building beliefs include:

- Things are always working out for me.
- Universe/God/spirit always has my back.
- Everything happens for a reason, and I trust that clarity will come someday after I leave this relationship.
- With every contraction comes expansion.
- Just like the caterpillar in the dark, gooey cocoon, I may not know of the growth and beauty I will experience on the other side of this challenge.
- I am a survivor, and I will survive this.

- I am worthy of love, and this is not love.
- There are 7.5 billion people on this planet. There are multiple opportunities for love.

We also tend to cling to the intention of finding that perfect partner that will love us unconditionally. We have stories about finding our soul mate, or the Christian marriage vow of "till death do us part." We place so much value on relationships with others that we usually forget about the most important relationship, which is the relationship with ourselves. What if your relationship with yourself and your inner child was the single most important relationship? What if your intention was to have compassion for your own heart, your own wounds, and your own healing, what would change? Most people who have been hurt by a narcissist have learned to turn their compassion in the wrong direction and MUST learn to return it to themselves. Can self-love, self-respect, and self-protection be your intention? What about the intention to stop betraying and abandoning yourself? What would be different if you came first instead of this relationship or your partner?

Insight

The Merriam-Webster dictionary defines insight as: *the power or act of seeing into a situation, the act or result of apprehending the inner nature of things or of seeing intuitively, the ability to understand people and situations in a very clear way, an understanding of the true nature of something.* The entire purpose of this book is to increase your insight, which is crucial if you want to protect yourself from abusive relationships. For this step in the LISTEN method, you must focus on two specific areas to increase your insight, external and internal red flags.

1. **Identify the external red flags.** Knowledge is power. Increase your awareness of personality disorders and pathology. Refer to the "external red flags" section of this book for this. You don't need to become an expert but knowing the costume the devil wears will decrease your chances of dancing with him or her. Here are a few refreshers:

- Does this person have qualities of a narcissist, sociopath, or psychopath?
- Do they seem to think they are special or superior to others?
- Did they move fast in the beginning of the relationship?
- How do they refer to their exes or past relationships? Is it always someone else's fault? Are all the exes "crazy?"
- Do you see two sides to this person, like Jekyll and Hyde?
- Does this person sabotage your plans or your successful or celebratory moments?
- Are you experiencing gaslighting, or just feel confused after conversations with them?
- Do you see the cycle of narcissistic abuse? (Idealize, Devalue, Discard)
- Do you see the DARVO cycle? (Deny, Attack, Reverse Victim & Offender)
- Does this person have patterns of instability in jobs or other relationships?
- Does this person walk their talk?

2. **Identify internal red flags.** In order to identify the internal red flags of a toxic relationship, it's important to pay attention to four key areas: mind, body, emotion, and spirit. Each has a different language, yet they are

interconnected. It will serve you well to spend more time and energy on developing your ability to listen to these internal systems than to get stuck spinning in Google searches trying to identify whether your partner is a narcissist. These systems don't care about a diagnosis. They will tell you what is right or wrong for you. Here are a few refreshers on internal red flags:

- Are you experiencing cognitive dissonance?
- Are there signs you are experiencing a trauma bond?
- Do you have any symptoms of PTSD (refer to chapter 7)?
- Are you experiencing fight, flight, freeze, or fawning responses frequently with your partner (see chapter 7)?
- Are you experiencing common stress-related physical symptoms (see chapter 9)?
- Have you identified your attachment style, and if so, are you feeling it activated (see chapter 8)?
- Are you walking on eggshells with your partner?
- Do you experience extreme highs and lows in the relationship?
- Do you find yourself ruminating about things that occurred or feeling suspicious of your partner's behaviors?
- If you are an empath or intuitive, are you feeling energetically drained around this person? Or are you noticing that you feel more disconnected from your intuition (likely because of trauma)?

3. **Notice your body:** This step involves building your interoceptive awareness. Learning to listen to your body will improve your ability to read and respond to your internal and external environment (and partners). As we learned in a previous chapter, interoceptive awareness is

the ability to identify, access, understand, and respond appropriately to internal signals and sensations in the body. Remember chronic trauma can lead to decreased interoceptive awareness, which leads to more difficulties identifying and managing your emotional state and responding to your environment (i.e., your abusive relationship). Much of our interoceptive awareness is unconscious, but with practice, we can increase our conscious awareness of our internal states.

Remember the frog in the saucepan analogy? If we apply this concept of interoceptive awareness to this poor little frog, it might be easier to understand. A healthy frog who isn't living with constant trauma inducing stress may find its way into a boiling pot of water and her interoceptive awareness says "OUCH! This is hot! I'm getting out of here!" and she jumps out of the pot to save herself. This frog's body senses the heat, and the frog's brain translates this heat into a message that says "You're in danger! Leave now!"

In contrast, let's imagine this poor little frog who is experiencing constant trauma responses because her partner is a narcissist. Her nervous system has created an internal protective buffer so that her body has essentially numbed itself to avoid feeling so much pain all of the time. This poor little frog is living in a pot of slowly heating water. She doesn't recognize the water is beginning to boil since her interoceptive awareness is compromised due to stress. Her brain isn't registering the heat nor the danger she is in. She eventually meets her demise because she is so disconnected from the red flags in her body that could have alerted her to this impending doom.

You may refer to earlier chapters on trauma and disease for more detailed insight on physical red flags, however, here are a few questions you can explore to tune in to the messages of your body:

- Check in with all five senses: touch, taste, smell, sight, hearing. What are you noticing with each sense?
- Does my heart rate increase at times of stress or when I anticipate an argument or fight, or when my partner enters the house or the room?
- Do I experience frequent diarrhea, especially in connection to stressful interactions with my partner?
- Do I experience insomnia?
- Are my muscles tense, especially when I'm near my partner?
- Do I sweat when I'm feeling stressed?
- Do I feel panicky or jittery frequently?
- Do I feel butterflies in my stomach?
- Am I feeling frozen or disconnected from my body?
- Have I ever felt like I'm watching events happen from outside of my body, or like things aren't real?
- Am I clenching my jaw or grinding my teeth?
- Do I experience a startle response (feeing jumpy or startled over noises, movements, or reactions from your partner or the environment around you)?
- Have I gained or lost significant weight since I've been in this relationship?
- Am I having any new physical symptoms or diseases since being in the relationship?

Activities that can help build interoceptive awareness include yoga (especially slower paced, mindful practices such as yin or restorative yoga), mindfulness practices, breathing exercises, and exercises that involves large muscles of your body. Therapists trained in MABT (Mindful Awareness in Body-Oriented Therapy), Somatic Experiencing, and Sensorimotor Psychotherapy can also help with this process.

4. **Notice your emotions:** Emotions can be tricky to identify, as people have differing levels of emotional awareness. Your attachment style, trauma, and the environment in which you were raised can play a part in how well you can identify, understand, and express your emotional states. Some questions to explore include:

- Do I feel depressed or down most of the time?
- Do I have difficulty sleeping or sleep too much (this can be a sign of depression)?
- Do I feel like I have no energy, motivation, or joy anymore?
- Do I feel fearful much of the time?
- Do I feel surprised by my angry responses or notice I didn't seem to get so angry before I met this partner?
- Do I feel intense periods of happiness and love, mixed with sadness, fear, anger, insecurity, etc.?
- Do I feel emotionally numb?
- Do I feel better when my partner is away from me?
- Do I feel constantly on edge, nervous, or anxious?
- Do I experience panic attacks?
- Do I feel ashamed for things I do or allow in this relationship?
- Do I feel embarrassed by my partner's actions around others?
- Do I experience strong feelings of anxiety when I think about leaving my partner or my partner leaving me?

Your emotions are powerful messengers but can also be triggered by trauma and events from our past. It is helpful to pay attention to your emotional state by also checking in with your thoughts and physical sensations to grasp the full context of a situation. For example, someone with PTSD may startle and experience overwhelming fear when they hear a loud bang, thinking they are in danger, but then realize the noise was only a door slamming, and they are not actually in danger, therefore the emotion of fear is incongruent with the situation.

5. **Notice your thoughts.** Our thoughts are powerfully intertwined with our physical and emotional state. What we think can influence the way we feel, and what we feel in our bodies can also lead to powerful emotions and thoughts. One of the single most important techniques you can develop to manage your thinking, so it doesn't manage you, is to become an observer of your thoughts. Also called *metacognition*, this simply means *you can think about how you think*.

Many of us, especially people who've experienced trauma or attachment wounds, also have a critical internal voice that is shaming, belittling, and outright cruel. By the way, we are not born with this voice. It is developed over time thanks to the trauma and pain caused by our parents, families, peers, social media, and the world we live in. For most of you, this voice is so internalized that you may not even recognize it is a product of your environment, and not your truth.

Your goal is to become a witness to the critical voice and identify it as such. This might go something like this: You start thinking "I'm such an idiot. I can't believe I did that!" Instead of allowing this inner dialogue to continue, you can pause and tell yourself, "there's that critical voice again, telling me that I'm an idiot. I'm not going to let it hurt me. I am human and it is ok to make mistakes." This is so important when you're dealing with an abusive partner, as they have likely been adding many negative messages to that inner critical voice.

Here are some thoughts and their related behaviors in relation to a pathological love relationship to help you increase metacognition:

- Am I experiencing cognitive dissonance, with conflicting thoughts such as "I love him/I fear him?"
- Is my self-talk more negative, demeaning, critical, and hurtful toward myself, and has it grown worse since I've been in this relationship?
- Do I tell myself I'm not good enough?
- Do I find myself denying or minimizing my needs, my opinions, wants, or desires?
- How do I act with this person? Am I authentic or do I change who I am to seek approval or keep the peace?
- Do I over apologize or find myself obsessing over what I did wrong?
- Am I overexplaining or justifying my actions?
- Am I hiding things or lying to avoid a fight?
- Do I think about setting a boundary but talk myself out of it?
- Am I constantly wondering if they are cheating on me?
- Do I ever wish my partner would die because I think it's the only way out?

- Do my thoughts have themes of hopelessness?
- Have I had suicidal thoughts?
- Am I actively denying things I have witnessed or have good reason to suspect? (i.e., seeing sexual texts on partner's phone from another woman but writing it off as nothing, making excuses for bad behavior, focusing and fantasizing about the good times yet ignoring the bad times in the relationship).

Becoming a witness to your thoughts is a powerful method to increase self-awareness, emotional regulation, and can improve your decision-making. Remember to pay attention to any signs of cognitive dissonance as you learn to observe your thoughts, as CD is the #1 red flag of a pathological love relationship.

6. **Notice your spirit or energy.** Depending on your spiritual beliefs, this may not apply to you. However, if you are someone who identifies as an empath, intuitive, highly sensitive person, or have spiritual or religious beliefs, this is another area in which you can increase your insight. Questions to ask yourself include:

- Do I feel drained when I'm around my partner?
- Do I feel energized when I'm away from my partner?
- Does my mood drastically shift when I'm around my partner, or does it match their mood?
- Have I been prohibited from following my spiritual or religious practices?
- Have I been criticized or demeaned because of them?
- Do I feel like I've lost touch with my higher self, the universe, God, spirit, etc.?

- Am I living in a way that is congruent to my spiritual beliefs when I'm in this relationship?
- Do I feel angry at or abandoned by God, the universe, etc.?
- Do I doubt intuitive messages about my partner because of cognitive dissonance?
- Do I feel disconnected from my intuition?
- Do I get intuitive red flags from one or more of my "clair" abilities about the relationship but ignore it?

Again, building your awareness in all of these areas will create a stronger relationship with yourself, leading to more confidence in your ability to identify, trust, and act upon red flags.

SANCTUARY

Your next goal is to create a "sanctuary" for yourself where you can experience refuge, safety, and space so you can foster an ideal environment for effective LISTENing. "Sanctuary" is defined as a place where someone or something is protected or given shelter, and also refers to the most sacred, holy part of a building, church, or temple (Merriam-Webster, 2022). Not only do you need physical distance between you and your partner, but you also need to imagine your mind, heart, body, and spirit as that of a sanctuary. It is your sacred, private space that needs to be treated as such. When your boundaries have been violated repeatedly, this step may seem impossible. However, with some imagination and creativity you can create your own sense of sanctuary.

My narcissistic partner followed me into the bathroom constantly. His constant need for my focus and attention on him drained the life force out of me. I didn't even have the most basic space available to me- the privacy and autonomy to escape to the bathroom. My time was dictated by his needs to talk about his concerns or to engage in his favorite activities or hobbies. He picked fights when I was falling asleep, interrupting even that most basic need for "space." He wouldn't allow me to wear makeup if we were "in nature," and tried to dictate little things like which sunglasses I should wear on a hike in an attempt to control the physical space of my body. He would call me between my therapy sessions, right on the dot, when I had five minutes to breathe, eat, use the bathroom, check emails, write my treatment notes, and ask for support for something he was stressed about. Sometimes this could happen every single hour of my day. This intrusion into the minute space of my being felt like a slow whittling away of my humanity. I needed a sanctuary like I needed air.

Consider all of the ways you need to feel safe, including physical, mental, emotional, or spiritual. When you are living with or in close contact with a toxic partner, your body, mind, heart, and spirit are under constant attack. As we've learned, the body will remain in a constant state of hypervigilance, bracing for the next battle. When your brain experiences this chronic trauma state, it cannot access the parts of it that can help you analyze, strategize, and plan your way out. You are focused on survival. Finding even the most basic moments of safety and space can give you glimpses into your reality, ultimately improving your clarity about the relationship.

If you are living with your partner, this can be the most challenging. Remember the concepts from Maslow's Hierarchy, and the importance of safety? If your physical safety or life is in danger, this should be your first priority. Intimate partner violence does not get better over time, it only gets worse and more dangerous. In this situation, literal physical space is necessary as soon as possible. If you aren't experiencing physical abuse or threats, you may not have the immediate urgency to leave. However, you may feel like your partner is constantly watching and controlling every move. Alternatively, you may have a partner who ignores you, but you still can't seem to escape the constant heaviness and presence of them.

Here are some ways to create "sanctuary" in your life so you can reclaim your sovereignty and autonomy:

- Keep a secret, hidden journal where you journal about your experiences. Journaling is incredibly helpful in pathological love relationships, as it can help you remember the crazy making incidents and gaslighting. It also gives you the ability to reflect on your experiences over time so you can see a pattern, and just how long you've endured the abuse. *Please notice how journaling makes you feel. It can be triggering for some if you are rehashing traumatic events. If it feels triggering, listing experiences, vs. free journaling can be more emotionally regulating.
- Take an intentional shower or a bath alone. Connect with your thoughts, feelings, body, and spirit. LISTEN to yourself, not your partner, in this moment.
- Improve your relationship with your sacred body to see how it is feeling. Set an alert on your phone to remind you to check in with your body throughout the day. What do you notice? Aches, pain, numbness? Trauma responses? This is your space. Get to know it well.

- Set boundaries wherever and whenever you safely can do so.
- Is there a safe or quiet space in your home? It may be your closet, garage, or bathroom. Any space will do, just to provide a physical separation from your partner.
- Take walks alone- a lot of them.
- Yoga, even if simply doing some poses at home on your own or through a YouTube video can be very helpful.
- Meditate daily.
- Create an altar- your sacred space- with a candle, special objects, crystals, or anything that reminds you to go within.
- Put metaphorical reminders around the house or in the phone that remind you of your strength, your intention, and to LISTEN. It could be an image of a strong woman, an animal, or spiritual figure that gives you strength and inspiration. Your partner will have no idea what these mean, but you will.
- If you like crystals, sage, and woo-woo things, sage your space and use crystals such as black obsidian and black tourmaline for protection.
- If you are an empath or intuitive, you can imagine a grounding cord coming from your hips all the way to the center of the earth. Imagine your aura bubble around you, extending about two feet around you on all sides. Frequently tune in to your aura bubble to clear it, imagining all negative or foreign energy dropping down the grounding cord into the center of the earth. Imagine a shield of protection around your bubble.
- If you have a trusted friend or family member who can listen without judgment, reach out and share your story.
- Protect the space of your body by seeking medical help. If you are experiencing health issues and have the resources

to seek help, please do so. In my experience, many of the stress-related symptoms associated with trauma are often overlooked by western medicine. Acupuncturists, nutritionists, naturopaths or functional medicine provider can work wonders with these conditions.

- Ideally, find a therapist *just for you*. If you don't have financial means to access therapy, there are usually community mental health centers, university counseling centers and non-profits who provide low-cost therapy. However, it is extremely important to be selective with your therapist and make sure they have experience AND knowledge in working with pathological love relationships or narcissistic abuse AND trauma. Remember therapists are bound by strict laws of confidentiality. This can be your safe space to talk about everything.
- **Do NOT go to couples therapy if you suspect or know your partner is a narcissist or pathological partner. This is not a safe space.** Right now, we are focusing on you only. We'll discuss this more in the final chapter, *Resources for Help and Healing*.
- If you are in physical danger, the most important step is to leave or cut ties as soon as possible.

Translate & Trust

Once you've listened with intention, increased your insight, and created the ideal sanctuary for this LISTENing practice, the next steps are to learn how to translate the messages you're receiving, and then of course, to trust them. For many of you, this will be the hardest part, and it may be an area where you need more support. It takes time to learn the language of your body, especially if you've spent your life, or a prolonged period of time disconnecting from it. Remember starting with an intention of curiosity and openness is key.

You can start with simple, explorative questions, and you can reference all you've learned about trauma in this book. Over time, as you befriend your body, you will become better at translating and trusting its language. Sometimes, we may have a hunch, a suspicion, or a physical feeling but will have no ability to translate it. Try not to overanalyze these feelings. The main point is you connect the sensation or hunch with a certain person, behavior, interaction, or environment. If it feels off in your body, that is your signal that is alerting you to stay aware. Instead of ignoring, dismissing, or rationalizing the signal, we LISTEN. We explore. We get curious. We become detectives. We do NOT abandon ourselves in that moment.

If you have childhood trauma or anything but a secure attachment, translating these nudges can be challenging. Early trauma and attachment wounds are often considered "developmental traumas." This means the trauma occurred during a stage of your childhood emotional, mental, and physical development. When this happens, we can become emotionally stuck in that developmental stage, even though our bodies continue to age.

For example, as children, we are normally egocentric, or self-centered. This doesn't mean that children are narcissistic. This is healthy, normal egocentrism. A child's brain has not developed the capacity to realize there is a world outside of it. If your dad comes home from work in a bad mood when you're five years old, you may believe you did something to cause the bad mood. You have no idea he has another life at work all day, separate from the one you share with him, and his mood was caused by a bad day at the office. If you grew up in a dysfunctional home, experiencing trauma, your brain may not have been able to work through this developmental stage of egocentrism. Therefore, you could be a forty-five-year-old person who is still having five-year-old egocentric reactions to the people and situations around you. You could experience this as feeling responsible for your partner's bad mood without recognizing it could have nothing to do with you.

What this means is our ability to translate our internal red flags can be somewhat off since there is a tendency for us to become egocentric in stressful or traumatic moments. When this happens, we may believe whatever negative interaction we are experiencing with another person is somehow about us. *What did I do? Was something I said too much? Did I do something wrong? I shouldn't have said that! I really am not good enough.* When it becomes about you, you may dismiss the red flag you just received because of this egocentric response of wondering what you did to cause the behavior that resulted in the red flag in the first place. Once again, we see the detrimental results of living under the influence of trauma.

What can you do about this? First of all, increase your insight and awareness. Again, we are trying to become objective observers of our experiences. When you know yourself better, you can begin to see these patterns. You can stop and hear the negative self-talk, the doubt, and the dismissal of your experiences in your head. A skilled therapist can also help you begin to externalize this self-talk and raise your awareness of your egocentric or trauma influenced perceptions.

Trust takes time. Think of these internal messages as a small child inside of you who kept raising their hand, trying to speak up and get your attention, but you ignored them. At some point, the child might have just given up, or is just very quiet. You may need to coax this child back into a place of power. Your body will give you the cues no matter what, however it is this voice inside that needs to be heard. When you begin to trust the cues, you will notice them more often. When you act upon them, you will increase your faith that they don't lie.

It is time to place your trust in you and stop betraying yourself. You deserve your trust so much more than someone who is abusing you. Give your instincts, hunches, and gut feelings the benefit of the doubt instead of giving it to an abusive partner. Trust your inner child when they say "I'm scared. I need us to leave NOW." Your experience is THE LAW. Your feelings are real. If you have a problem with something, that is ALL that matters. Choose you.

EMPOWERED ACTION

Once you incorporate the first four steps of the LISTEN method, your self-awareness will improve, nonetheless awareness without action will not save you. Taking action requires courage and confidence in yourself. Taking action means you are no longer going to put up with this abuse. You are no longer going to betray yourself. You will no longer allow yourself to be a victim, and instead you will rise up and out of the abuse. You do not owe anyone an explanation or justification for leaving a relationship that is hurting you.

Taking action can include a myriad of steps, depending on your situation. Some examples include:

- Setting a boundary, big or small
- Not engaging in an argument
- Stop apologizing for things you didn't do
- Contacting a divorce attorney if you're married
- Going to therapy
- Creating a secret bank account where you can save money to leave
- Protecting your children from further abuse by leaving
- Forgiving yourself
- Daily acts of self-care
- Eating healthy and trying to improve physical health
- Putting your inner child first and telling them you will no longer subject her to this abuse
- Protecting your children from more abuse or witnessing the abuse of you
- Leaving

Using Maslow's Hierarchy can be a useful tool to help you determine your priorities when taking action but remember it is simply a tool and is not the only way to do this. Some people may need to focus on physically exiting a dangerous relationship by going to a domestic violence shelter and finding immediate safety and shelter. Focusing on therapy or self-compassion at that time is nearly impossible as your energy is focused on survival. Another person may be able to go to therapy and start implementing strategies to build their confidence or to begin healing from trauma because they are in a situation where their basic needs are being met. The key here is to take action, no matter how big or small, once you have realized you are experiencing red flags. Awareness without action is a betrayal of yourself and your inner child.

NURTURE AND HEAL

Every time I have left a relationship with a narcissist, I have felt bloodied and bruised, even if my body lacked the physical evidence of my injuries. Every single part of my being was worn down and exhausted. This step is vital, and sometimes overlooked if we are not paying attention to the underlying trauma that has developed. You may leave the relationship and find yourself in a stressful financial, legal, parenting, or other situation that creates more stress. It may feel impossible to find the time to take care of yourself.

Please listen to me. **You must not bypass this step, ever.** Skipping over this step will inevitably lead to more stress on your body, mind, heart, and spirit. Furthermore, if you later proceed to date other people, you may risk ending up with another abusive, toxic partner.

If you have left a toxic relationship, I strongly recommend you refrain from dating until you have spent some dedicated time working on healing and reconnecting with yourself. Trauma does not heal overnight. Exposing your vulnerable heart and psyche to new partners when you have not done your healing work is an invitation for more predators. That may sound extreme, but I speak from decades of experience, both personally and professionally. If you want to break this pattern, you MUST engage in some healing first. Reading blogs, following your favorite YouTuber, or simply reading a book about narcissism is unlikely to change the deeper trauma you've experienced.

If you can't imagine staying single and have the desire to find a new partner within weeks or months after a pathological love relationship, this should be your first red flag that you should NOT date right now. If this is the case, I would highly recommend you make a decision to put your relationship with yourself first. Nurturing yourself, instead of betraying yourself is the goal. Here are some ideas to get started:

- Date you. Get to know your interests, your hobbies, your likes and dislikes. Spend time alone, learning to explore and tolerate the feelings of loneliness. Take a solo trip somewhere. Eat alone in a nice restaurant or cook a nice dinner for yourself every Friday night. Get massages. Spend time in nature.
- Get to know your inner child. What do they need or want? Children aren't searching for partners. They are searching for love, protection, attention, belonging and validation. Give your inner child what they need. It may feel silly or childlike, but that's ok. You may find you need naps, or playful, creative activities like creating art, singing, dancing, or playing games. Children need friends, not romance.
- Reclaim what you lost in the relationship. Did you live together? Do the things you weren't allowed to do, like decorate, get messy or get organized. Buy that cute chair you admired or go on that backpacking trip in Costa Rica. You must learn to reclaim your sense of self in the absence of a partner's influence. You must find you. You must give your inner child a chance to be heard, be seen, and to be protected. Buy a new bed or bedding. Sage your house. Dress the way you want. Reignite lost friendships.
- Go to trauma focused therapy because you have experienced trauma. Trauma is not healed by reading a self-help

book or changing your thoughts. It is also not healed by finding a new partner. If you want to create lasting change, I cannot emphasize enough the power of working with a therapist who specializes in body-focused trauma therapy and understands these types of relationships.
- Heal the body. As we've learned, most people who've experienced trauma will have at least some degree of stress-related symptoms in the body. Depending on the severity of your symptoms, it is crucial to find medical or holistic support for your health. Acupuncture, nutrition, functional or naturopathic medicine, yoga, meditation are all powerful healing modalities that incorporate mind, body, heart, and spirit.
- Spiritual and energetic work can be helpful if you believe in this. Reiki, prayer and connection with your religious beliefs, breathwork, cord cutting, meditation, mindfulness practices, shamanic healings, and psychedelic or plant medicine ceremonies can be powerful healing tools.

LISTENing is the key to breaking this pattern and healing. We must stop betraying ourselves and return the compassion to the person that deserves it. Your body holds incredible wisdom and can be your guiding north star if you simply learn to listen, honor your truth, and act upon it.

CONCLUSION

You may be asking yourself, ok, so now what? How do I heal? How do I trust in love again? Please think of this book as the first step of your healing journey. It is here to help you identify whether you are in an abusive relationship, and how to prevent one from happening. As we've learned, most survivors of pathological love relationships find themselves paralyzed in indecision due to cognitive dissonance and trauma and can waste precious months and years of their lives wondering if they are being abused or if it is somehow their fault.

This book is your wakeup call. Awareness is the first step, whether it's in gaining clarity that you are being abused, or as the first step you can take in dating and vetting a new partner. You can't heal a wound if you are unaware of its presence. You now have information that can serve as relationship armor. You've learned the answers you seek when questioning whether a relationship is right for you lies both within and outside of you. As a red flag detective, you now know the importance of searching for the external signs of pathology and the internal cues of danger.

Most importantly, you've learned you have a powerful inner guidance system. Identifying whether someone is pathological or diagnosable is never as important as what your gut is telling you. Don't rack your brain if you can't identify whether you're being gaslighted or manipulated. What matters most is how you *feel* when you are with this person. How does your body react? What thoughts and feelings do you experience? How do you behave with this person? Do you feel safe to be yourself? Have you lost yourself in this relationship? You have an invaluable tool that can help you navigate your life decisions and ultimately protect you from abusive, unhealthy relationships. You must simply learn to listen, trust, and act upon these messages that are held in the sacred container of your body.

You've learned some people are more vulnerable to these toxic relationships than others. If you have the super traits of agreeableness and conscientiousness, are an empath or HSP, or if you have an anxious attachment or history of trauma, you are particularly vulnerable. Regardless of what got you into the relationship, once you're in and your brain has been hijacked by trauma, you will be challenged to make rational, wise decisions. Remember the problem solving, analytical part of your brain is off-line, and you are living in survival mode when you are experiencing this abuse. Survival mode will keep you stuck in your present moment, as that is its purpose. It won't help you see into the future, and how this relationship might be affecting your overall well-being. This is why leaving an abusive relationship and addressing your trauma is incredibly important. You cannot begin to heal if you are under constant threat.

We've also learned the Jekyll and Hyde personality and erratic behavior of a toxic partner can create cognitive dissonance, and ultimately a trauma bond that can keep you paralyzed in indecision about whether to leave. Recognizing that you are experiencing trauma bond dynamics and cognitive dissonance is THE #1 RED FLAG that should never be ignored. While you may not be able to make clear decisions about the relationship, simply recognizing you are experiencing this dynamic is a step. It is highly recommended that you engage in therapy and limit or end contact with your abuser if this is occurring.

Once you've identified the red flags, you can decide how to implement this information into your life and relationships by ascertaining where you are and what you need. Using Maslow's Hierarchy, you can pinpoint where to begin your healing journey. Most importantly, we've identified six steps in the LISTEN method to give you a road map to build your awareness and self-protective abilities.

If you have noticed a pattern of ignoring red flags in your relationships, you may feel a sense of regret, guilt, or even shame. Please remember you are human. While it is now your responsibility to take control of your safety and healing, it is not your fault you were manipulated and abused by a toxic person. It is not your fault the love-bombing, empty promises, and highs and lows entangled you in a web of deceit that appeared to be a relationship but was actually an experience of domestic abuse. Please forgive yourself. It is human to want and need love and connection. It is human to trust, to forgive, and to believe in the goodness of others. It is ok to be right where you are in this moment.

You might be wondering if I'm still with a narcissist. Today I can happily say the answer is *no*. It took work and courage to get to a place where I could recognize the reality of my relationships, heal my trauma and cognitive dissonance, and choose to break free sooner rather than later. There were times in the past where it took much longer than I wish it had for me to leave a narcissistic partner. Over time, I learned to trust the signals in my body, mind, heart, and spirit when I saw something was off in my relationship. Despite deep heartbreak, feelings of loss and regret, the life challenges of a breakup, the shame for missing the signs… again, I knew none of it mattered. I listened and acted upon the signs I received. I chose me. I chose safety. I chose self-respect. I chose to stop betraying the voice inside that was crying out for protection. I chose freedom and health. You can do this too. Listening is a muscle. It strengthens with every use.

By sharing my "hindsight is 20/20" moment, I hope others can learn and grow from my experiences. What is different now, and what helps me feel strong in my ability to detect future narcissists is my strong relationship with myself, my body, and my truth. I am attached to an outcome of healthy, self-protective boundaries and a joy-filled life (whether I am single or partnered) more than I am attached to an outcome of finding a loving, healthy partner in my life. I am intent on listening to my instincts, my intuition, and my trauma responses. I have turned my empathy and compassion inward, while maintaining my empathic, openhearted sensitivity for others. I gave up the misidentified belief that I was codependent and have become a keen observer of my super traits. I value them, as they make me capable of creating strong, loving relationships, but I now know how to manage them so I can protect myself from toxic people.

THE PLEDGE OF SELF-PROTECTION

If the red flags in this book have resonated with you, you are being abused. This is your call to action. Seek help and do it now. In order to move forward and strengthen your ability to tune in, increase your internal awareness, and set boundaries to protect yourself, keep this Pledge of Self-Protection in mind:

I honor my body and its sacred language.

I honor my intuition.

I honor my inner child and learn to listen to their voice.

I honor my boundaries.

I have a right to set boundaries, even if they make others uncomfortable.

I honor and use my voice.

I am powerful.

I deserve compassion.

I must have empathy for myself and my experiences as much as I empathize with others.

I am human.

It is ok to make mistakes.

I forgive myself for not seeing the red flags earlier.

I forgive myself for ignoring the red flags.

I forgive myself for betraying myself.

I am enough.

I am worth loving.

I love myself.

We must work together to end this pattern of toxic, pathological love relationships. True love should never leave emotional, psychological, spiritual, or physical scars. May this book be a step in your journey to healing, wholeness, freedom, and safety. Like a piece of Kintsugi, may a healing, golden web weave itself around your heart, and may you trust that love will someday be a place of safety, growth, and refuge. Most of all, LISTEN and TRUST yourself. You always know your truth.

RESOURCES FOR HELP & HEALING

FINDING A THERAPIST

If you have endured a pathological love relationship and have symptoms of trauma, I highly recommend you find a licensed mental health therapist who has experience and training in working with both trauma and pathological love relationships. Some therapists may not know about PLRs but may have experience working with narcissistic abuse or domestic violence. Admittedly, this is a specialized area, so you may be challenged to find someone in your area. Don't be afraid to interview several therapists and ask questions about their knowledge of this topic.

Couples therapy: DO NOT attend couples therapy if you believe your partner has a personality disorder. This can be further damaging and even dangerous. Many therapists can fall prey to a charismatic, manipulative pathological partner and can unwittingly gaslight you or embolden your partner in their abuse.

Coaching: Beware of survivor coaches who are well-meaning, however, lack clinical training and experience in working with trauma and PLRs. Being a "trauma-informed coach" is NOT the same as being a trauma therapist and should not be confused. Working with an inexperienced coach or therapist can lead to further re-traumatization and worsening of your symptoms.

Trauma therapy: The most important thing to look for if you cannot find a therapist who is specifically trained in and knowledgeable of PLRs or narcissistic abuse is a trauma therapist. Unfortunately, there are also many therapists in the field who represent themselves as "trauma therapists," yet lack specific trauma training. The most effective trauma therapists should have training or certification in modalities that focus on the body, or somatic types of processing. Here are some somatic focused trauma specialties that can be helpful:

- EMDR: (Eye Movement Desensitization and Reprocessing). This is one of the most highly researched, evidence backed effective treatment modalities for trauma.
- Somatic Experiencing
- Sensorimotor Psychotherapy
- Internal Family Systems (IFS) therapy
- Brainspotting
- Mindful Awareness in Body-oriented Therapy (MABT)

DOMESTIC VIOLENCE SHELTERS & LEGAL ASSISTANCE
- Your local domestic violence shelter
- Domestic Violence Support Hotline: 1-800-799-SAFE (7233) or Text "START" to 88788
- www.thehotline.org

- https://www.narcissistabusesupport.com/legal-aid/ To help find legal assistance
- http://www.loveisrespect.org/legal-help/restraining-orders/ Information on restraining orders
- https://www.onemomsbattle.com Support for divorcing pathological partners
- https://narcissistabusesupport.com/narcissist-abuse-support-groups/ State by state list of support groups

RECOMMENDED WEBSITES
- www.chellipumphrey.com For coaching and therapy
- www.saferelationshipsmagazine.com The Institute for Relational Harm Reduction and Safe Relationships Magazine
- www.survivortreatment.com Association for NPD/Psychopathy Survivor Treatment, Research & Education
- www.narcissistabusesupport.com General website with many resources
- www.leeharris.com (Narcissists vs. empaths online course)
- www.doctor-ramani.com Dr. Ramani's YouTube channel contains helpful insight about NPD and narcissistic abuse

BOOKS ABOUT NARCISSISTIC ABUSE, TRAUMA, ATTACHMENT, AND PLRS
- *Women Who Love Psychopaths: Inside the Relationships of Inevitable Harm with Psychopaths, Sociopaths, & Narcissists* by Sandra L. Brown, MA, and Jennifer L. Young, LMHC
- *How to Spot a Dangerous Man* by Sandra L. Brown, MA
- *Why Can't I Just Leave? A Guide to Waking Up and Walking Out of A Pathological Love Relationship* by Kristen Milstead, PhD
- *Invisible Chains: Overcoming Coercive Control in Your Relationship* by Dr. Lisa Aronson Fontes.

- *Out of the Fog Moving from Confusion to Clarity After Narcissistic Abuse* by Dana Morningstar.
- *The New Science of Narcissism: Understanding One of the Greatest Psychological Challenges of Our Time- And What You Can Do about It* by Keith Campbell and Carolyn Crist.
- *The Highly Sensitive Person: How to Thrive When the World Overwhelms You* by Elaine Aron.
- *The Empath's Survival Guide: Life Strategies for Sensitive People* by Judith Orloff.
- *The Betrayal Bond: Breaking Free of Exploitative Relationships* by Patrick J. Carnes.
- *Complex PTSD: From Surviving to Thriving: A Guide and Map for Recovering from Childhood Trauma* by Pete Walker.
- *Attached: The New Science of Adult Attachment and How It Can Help You Find-and Keep-Love* by Amir Levine and Rachel Heller.
- *When the Body Says No: The Cost of Hidden Stress* by Dr. Gabor Maté.
- *The Body Keeps the Score: Brain, Mind, And Body in The Healing of Trauma* by Bessel van der Kolk.

APPENDIX

INTRODUCTION

American Psychiatric Association. *Diagnostic and Statistical Manual of Mental Disorders (DSM-5)*. Washington, DC: APA Publishing, 2013.

Brown, Sandra L. *How to Spot a Dangerous Man before You Get Involved*. Alameda: Hunter House Publications, 2005.

Brown, Sandra L., and Jennifer Young. *Women Who Love Psychopaths: Inside the Relationships of Inevitable Harm with Psychopaths, Sociopaths & Narcissists*. 3rd ed. Balsam Grove: Mask Publishing, 2009–2018.

Campbell, Keith, and Carolyn Crist. *The New Science of Narcissism: Understanding One of the Greatest Psychological Challenges of Our Time- And What You Can Do about It*. Boulder: Sounds True, 2020.

National Center for Injury Prevention and Control, Centers for Disease Control and Prevention. The National Intimate Partner and Sexual Violence Survey (NISVS): 2010 Summary Report by Michele Black, Kathleen Basile, Matthew Breiding, Sharon Smith, Mikel Walters, Melissa Merrick, Jieru Chen and Mark Stevens. Georgia, 2010. https://www.cdc.gov/violenceprevention/pdf/nisvs_report2010-a.pdf.

Sanz-García, Ana, Clara Gesteira, Jesus Sanz, and Maria Paz García-Vera. "Prevalence of Psychopathy in the General Adult Population: A Systematic Review and Meta-Analysis." *Frontiers in Psychology* 12, no. 661044(August 2021): https://doi: 10.3389/fpsyg.2021.661044.

Trzesniewski, Kali H., and M. Brent Donnellan. "Rethinking 'Generation Me': A Study of Cohort Effects from 1976–2006." *Perspectives on Psychological Science* 5, no. 1 (January 2010): 58–75. https://doi.org/10.1177/1745691609356789.

Twenge, Jean, and Keith Campbell. *The Narcissism Epidemic: Living in the Age of Entitlement.* New York: Simon & Shuster, 2009.

U.S. Department of Justice Statistics. Intimate Partner Violence, by Shannan Catalano. Washington, DC, 2012. https://bjs.ojp.gov/library/publications/intimate-partner-violence-1993-2010.

Vater, Aline, Steffen Moritz, and Stefan Roepk. "Does a Narcissism Epidemic Exist in Modern Western Societies? Comparing Narcissism and Self-Esteem in East and West Germany." *PLoS One* 13, no. 1 (January 2018): e0198386. https://doi.org/10.1371/journal.pone.0188287.

Yu, Ronggin, Alejo Nevado-Holgado, Yasmina Molero, Brian D'Onofrio, Henrik Larsson, Louise Howard, and Seena Fazel.

"Mental Disorders and Intimate Partner Violence Perpetrated by Men Towards Women: A Swedish Population-Based Longitudinal Study." *PLoS Medicine* 16, no. 12 (December 2019): e1002995.https://doi.org/10.1371/journal.pmed.1002995.

CHAPTER 1: RED FLAGS

Brown, Sandra, and Jennifer Young. *Women Who Love Psychopaths: Inside the Relationships of Inevitable Harm with Psychopaths, Sociopaths & Narcissists.* 3rd ed. Balsam Grove: Mask Publishing, 2009-2018.

Lufityanto, Galang, Chris Donkin, and Joel Pearson. "Measuring Intuition: Nonconscious Emotional Information Boosts Decision Accuracy and Confidence." *Psychological Science* 27, no. 5 (May 2016): 622-34. https://doi:10.1177/0956797616629403.

Merriam-Webster Dictionary Online. s.v. "red-flag (v.)." Accessed October 16, 2021.https://www.merriam-webster.com/dictionary/red-flag.

Orloff, Judith. *The Empath's Survival Guide: Life Strategies for Sensitive People.* Boulder: Sounds True, 2017.

CHAPTER 2: PATHOLOGY 101

American Psychiatric Association. *Diagnostic and Statistical Manual of Mental Disorders (DSM-5).* Washington, DC: APA Publishing, 2013.

Baumeister, Roy, Laura Smart, and Joseph Boden. "Relation of Threatened Egotism to Violence and Aggression: The Dark Side of High Self-Esteem." *Psychological Review* 103, no. 1 (January 1996): 5-33. doi: 10.1037/0033-295x.103.1.5.

Brummelman, Eddie, Jennifer Crocker, and Brad Bushman. "The Praise Paradox: When and Why Praise Backfires in Children with Low Self-Esteem." *Child Development Perspectives* 10, no. 2 (March 2016): 111–115. https://doi.org/10.1111/cdep.12171.

Glen O. Gabbard and the American Psychiatric Association. *Gabbard's Treatments of Psychiatric Disorders*. 5th ed. Washington, DC: American Psychiatric Publishing, 2014.

Hare, Robert D. "Psychopathy and Antisocial Personality Disorder: A Case of Diagnostic Confusion." *Psychiatric Times* 13, no. 2 (February 1996). https://www.psychiatrictimes.com/view/psychopathy-and-antisocial-personality-disorder-case-diagnostic-confusion.

Kaya, Suheda, Hanefi Yildirim, and Murad Atmaca. "Reduced Hippocampus and Amygdala Volumes in Antisocial Personality Disorder." *Journal of Clinical Neuroscience* 75, no. 4 (January 2020): 199-203. doi: 10.1016/j.jocn.2020.01.048.

Nenadic, Igor, Daniel Güllmar, Maren Dietzek, Kerstin Langbein, Johanna Steinke, and Christian Gader. "Brain Structure in Narcissistic Personality Disorder: A VBM and DTI Pilot Study." *Psychiatry Research: Neuroimaging* 231, no. 2 (February 2015): 184–86. doi:10.1016/j.pscychresns.2014.11.001.

Torgersen, Svenn, Sissel Lygren, Per Andersen, Ingunn Skre, Sidsel Onstad, Jack Edvardsen, KristianTambs, and Einar Kringlen. "A Twin Study of Personality Disorders." *Comprehensive Psychiatry* 41, no. 6 (May 2002): 416–425. https://doi.org/10.1053/comp.2000.16560.

Twenge, Jean, and Keith Campbell. *The Narcissism Epidemic: Living in the Age of Entitlement.* New York: Simon & Shuster, 2009.

CHAPTER 3: THE FACES OF NARCISSISM

American Psychiatric Association. *Diagnostic and Statistical Manual of Mental Disorders (DSM-5).* Washington, DC: APA Publishing, 2013.

Russ, Eric, Jonathan Shedler, Rebekah Bradley, and Drew Westen. "Refining the Construct of Narcissistic Personality Disorder: Diagnostic Criteria and Subtypes." *The American Journal of Psychiatry,* 165 no. 11 (November 2008): 1473–81. doi:10.1176/appi.ajp.2008.07030376.

CHAPTER 4: MINDFUCKERY

Freyd, Jennifer J. "Violations of Power, Adaptive Blindness, and Betrayal Trauma Theory." *Feminism & Psychology* 7 no. 1 (February 1997): 22–32. https://doi.org/10.1177%2F0959353597071004.

Thomas, Laura. "Gaslight and Gaslighting." *The Lancet.* 5, no. 2. (February 2018): 117–118. https://doi.org/10.1016/S2215-0366(18)30024-5.

CHAPTER 5: WHAT MAKES US VULNERABLE

Aron, Elaine. *The Highly Sensitive Person: How to Thrive When the World Overwhelms You.* New York: Broadway Books, 1987.

Beattie, Melody. *Codependent No More: How to Stop Controlling Others and Start Caring for Yourself.* Center City: Hazelden, 1986.

Brown, Sandra L. *How to Spot a Dangerous Man before You Get Involved.* Alameda: Hunter House Publications, 2005.

Brown, Sandra, and Jennifer Young. *Women Who Love Psychopaths: Inside the Relationships of Inevitable Harm with Psychopaths, Sociopaths & Narcissists*. 3rd ed. Balsam Grove: Mask Publishing, 2009–2018.

Orloff, Judith. *The Empath's Survival Guide: Life Strategies for Sensitive People*. Boulder: Sounds True, 2017.

Wegscheider-Cruse, Sharon. *Another Chance: Hope and Health for the Alcoholic Family*. Palo Alto: Science & Behavior Books, 1989.

CHAPTER 6: THE #1 RED FLAG

Brown, Sandra L., and Jennifer Young. *Women Who Love Psychopaths: Inside the Relationships of Inevitable Harm with Psychopaths & Narcissists*. 3rd ed. Balsam Grove: Mask Publishing, 2018.

Carnes, Patrick J. *The Betrayal Bond: Breaking Free of Exploitative Relationships*. Deerfield Beach: Health Communications Inc., 2019.

CHAPTER 7: THE BODY SPEAKS YOUR TRUTH:
THE LANGUAGE OF TRAUMA

American Psychiatric Association. *Diagnostic and Statistical Manual of Mental Disorders (DSM-5)*. Washington, DC: APA Publishing, 2013.

Brown, Sandra L. "When Your Walk Doesn't Match Your Talk: The Sensitive System of Survivors-A Series on Cognitive Dissonance." *Safe Relationships Magazine*. Article 3, 2017.

Brown, Sandra, and Jennifer Young. *Women Who Love Psychopaths: Inside the Relationships of Inevitable Harm with Psychopaths, Sociopaths & Narcissists*. 3rd ed. Balsam Grove: Mask Publishing, 2009–2018.

Merriam-Webster.com Dictionary, s.v. "cognitive dissonance (n.)." Accessed January 14, 2022. https://www.merriam-webster.com/dictionary/cognitive%20dissonance.

Schwartz, Arielle. "The Fawn Response in Complex PTSD." *Dr. Arielle Schwartz (blog).* March 9, 2021. https://drarielleschwartz.com/the-fawn-response-in-complex-ptsd-dr-arielle-schwartz/#.YeR6dFjMLop.

Walker, Pete. *Complex PTSD: From Surviving to Thriving: A Guide and Map for Recovering from Childhood Trauma.* Scotts Valley: CreateSpace Independent Publishing Platform, 2013.

CHAPTER 8: THE BODY SPEAKS YOUR TRUTH: THE LANGUAGE OF ATTACHMENT

Bowlby, John. *A Secure Base: Parent Child Attachment and Healthy Human Development.* New York: Basic Books, 1988.

Levine, Amir, and Rachel Heller. *Attached: The New Science of Adult Attachment and How It Can Help You Find-and Keep-Love.* New York: TarcherPerigee, 2012.

CHAPTER 9: THE BODY SPEAKS YOUR TRUTH: THE LANGUAGE OF DISEASE

Chandan, Joht Singh, Tom Thomas, Karim Raza, Caroline Bradbury-Jones, Julie Taylor, Siddhartha Bandyopadhyay, and Krishnarajah Nirantharakumar. "Intimate Partner Violence and the Risk of Developing Fibromyalgia and Chronic Fatigue Syndrome." *Journal of Interpersonal Violence* 36, no. 21-22 (November 2021): NP12279-98. https://doi.org/10.1177/0886260519888515.

Craig, A. D. *How Do You Feel? An Interoceptive Moment with Your Neurobiological Self.* Princeton: Princeton University Press, 2015.

Del Giudice, Marco, Bruce Ellis, and Elizabeth A Shirtcliff. "The Adaptive Calibration Model of Stress Responsivity." *Neuroscience and Biobehavioral Reviews* 35, no. 7 (2011): 1562–92. doi:10.1016/j.neubiorev.2010.11.007.

Gershon, Michael. *The Second Brain: A Groundbreaking New Understanding of Nervous Disorders of the Stomach and Intestine.* New York City: Harper Perennial, 1999.

Goleman, Daniel. *Emotional Intelligence: Why It Can Matter More Than IQ.* New York City: Random House Publishing, 2005.

Leserman, Jane, Douglas Drossman, Zhiming Li, Timothy Toomey, Ginette Nachman, and Louise Glogau. "Sexual and Physical Abuse History in Gastroenterology Practice." *Psychosomatic Medicine*: 58 no. 1 (January/February 1996): 4–15. doi: 10.1097/00006842-199601000-00002.

Maté, Gabor. *When the Body Says No: The Cost of Hidden Stress.* Toronto: Vintage Publishing, 2021.

McFarlane, Alexander C. "The Long-Term Costs of Traumatic Stress: Intertwined Physical and Psychological Consequences." *World Psychiatry* 9, no. 1 (February 2010): 3–10. doi:10.1002/j.2051-5545.2010.tb00254.x.

Parkin Kullmann, Jane, Susan Hayes, and Roger Pamphlett. "Are People with Amyotrophic Lateral Sclerosis (ALS) Particularly Nice? An International Online Case-Control Study of the Big

Five Personality Factors." *Brain and Behavior* 8, no. 10 (October 2018): e01119. https://doi.org/10.1002/brb3.1119.

Price, Cynthia, and Carol Hooven. "Interoceptive Awareness Skills for Emotion Regulation: Theory and Approach of Mindful Awareness in Body-Oriented Therapy (MABT)." *Frontiers in Psychology* 9, no. 798 (May 2018). https://doi.org/10.3389/fpsyg.2018.00798.

Schulz, Andre, and Claus Vögele. "Interoception and Stress." *Frontiers in Psychology*, no. 6 (July 2015): 993. https://doi.org/10.3389/fpsyg.2015.00993.

van der Kolk, Bessel. *The Body Keeps the Score: Brain, Mind, and Body in the Healing of Trauma*. City Of Westminster: Penguin Publishing Group, 2015.

CHAPTER 10: HEALING: THE FIRST STEPS
Maslow, Abraham. *Motivation and Personality*. 3rd edition. New York City: Pearson, 1997.

CHAPTER 11: HOW TO LISTEN
Itani, Omar. "5 Teachings from the Japanese Wabi Sabi Philosophy That Can Drastically Improve Your Life." *Omar Itani* (blog). April 23, 2021. https://www.omaritani.com/blog/wabi-sabi-philosophy-teachings.

Merriam-Webster. s.v. "insight (n.)." Accessed January 30, 2022. https://www.merriam-webster.com/dictionary/insight.

Merriam-Webster., s.v. "sanctuary (n.)." Accessed February 15, 2022. https://www.merriam-webster.com/dictionary/sanctuary.

ACKNOWLEDGMENTS

This book would not exist had it not been for generations of women who have endured abuse by their partners, families, communities, governments, and religions. I am grateful to the generations of women who have come before me and to those who will come after me for continuing to love despite your scars. I have been inspired by these fiercely strong women in my life: my mom, daughters, sister, aunts, niece, and grandmothers. I stand upon your shoulders and carry your strength in my bones. May we pass our collective strength on to those who need it right now.

I am deeply grateful for my daughters, Mila and Marley, for your grace and never-ending patience with me falling asleep on the couch every night in a sleep deprived, author's slumber. Thank you for inspiring me to be a better human being. This book and its message are for you. Always trust yourself.

To my sister, Andrea, thank you for always being my rock. I cannot thank you enough for your unconditional love, patience, support, and wisdom. Not only did you listen to me babble on about my relationships and this book a bajillion times, but you also made sure it got published. Thank you for holding my heart in your hands.

To Melissa Wolak and Candice Kingston, there are no words to describe the beautiful, synergistic friendship that has developed between us since our B-School mastermind days. This book would not be possible without your endless support, encouragement, and belief in me. I can't wait to see what the future holds for us!

Sandra Brown, I will be forever grateful for your generous time, support, and belief in me and my message. It is one of my deepest honors to have your blessing for this book. May the seeds of your life's work continue to spread and help every woman who has been harmed by a pathological partner, and hopefully someday, help us prevent this from happening at all.

To all of my family, friends, and colleagues who have believed in me and encouraged me to vulnerably share my story. Writing this book has been no small task, and I'm sure I've neglected you in this process. Your patience, faith, and support mean the world to me.

I owe a huge thank you to the women and men who shared their stories for this book. While your names are confidential, your vulnerability and strength will undoubtedly help others heal. Your courage is inspiring.

I share a special thank you to my dedicated beta readers who took the time out of their busy lives to pick through every sentence in this book. I seriously don't know how you did it. Melissa Wolak, Candice Kingston, Tierney Shaffer, and Colleen Sullivan, and Sandra Brown, I am forever grateful.

Eric Koester, I am so grateful for your passionate, brilliant, heart centered dedication to helping authors bring their stories to life. To Brian Bies and the teams at the Creator Institute and New Degree Press, thank you for providing a platform to help me share my story. Thank you for challenging the paradigm and bringing community publishing to the world. I am deeply grateful for my editors, Melody Delgado Lorbeer and Bianca daSilva for helping me believe in myself, my writing, and my story. There were many times I wanted to throw in the towel, however your reassurance, guidance, and wisdom held me up through the finish line.

This book was also made possible by a community of people who believed in me so fervently they pre-ordered their copies and helped promote the book before it even went to print. Thanks to you, many of whom gave input on the book title and cover. You are amazing, and as promised, you are in the book!

Jessica Abegg,
Nikki Aiello
Tanya Alpert
Bethany Barta
Kelly Bianucci
Mimi Blanch
Anne Charles
Kimber Chin
Debi Circle
Denise Cordner

Angela Coyle
Sybil Cummin
Kristen Dooley
Imogen Erickson
Donovan Garcia
Tiffany Garcia
Sharon Gold
Andrea, Scott, & Tristan Hansen
Pat Hansen

Elizabeth Hauptman
Jamie Heidbrink
Cynthia R Hodge
Rebecca Hubbard
Dr. Carrie Johansson
Debra Johnson
Jaelee Jones
Julie Keywell
Candice Kingston
Eric Koester
Carrie Ledford
Heather Mahoney
Rita Marquez
Tara Masterson
Jill Maxwell
Precious McKoy
Jamie McGinnis
Gennifer Morley
Rachel Neff
Tiffany Nichols

Michelle Ockman
Michelle Oviatt
Brian & Ella Pumphrey
Karla and Paul Pumphrey
Tormey Pumphrey
Carol Ribar
Jacqueline R Rivera
Val Savidge
Jessica Schaller
Tierney Shaffer
Holly Smith
Colleen Sullivan
Jennifer Tam
Jack Todaro
Amanda Vallero
Connie & Arlyn VanWinkle
Michelle Vos
Jalyn Webb
Melissa Wolak
Elizabeth Young

www.ingramcontent.com/pod-product-compliance
Lightning Source LLC
LaVergne TN
LVHW012012060526
838201LV00061B/4274